3ds Max 2018 - Getting Started with Standard Materials and Lights

Ravi Conor

and

Elizabeth VT

RISING POLYGON

Copyright © Rising Polygon

Book Code: RP14C

ISBN: 978-1975929350

Web: www.risingpolgon.co

Author Email: raveeoc@gmail.com

Contents

Acknowledgements

About the Author

Preface

Unit MT1 - Creating Textures in Photoshop MT1-1

  Non-destructive Editing MT1-1

    Adjustment Layers MT1-1

    Filtering with Smart Filter MT1-2

    Retouching on a Separate Layer MT1-3

    Nondestructive Crop MT1-4

    Masking MT1-4

    Blending Modes MT1-4

    Normal Category MT1-6

    Subtractive Category MT1-6

    Additive Category MT1-6

    Complex Category MT1-6

    Difference Category MT1-6

    HSL Category MT1-6

    High Pass Filter MT1-7

    Using Channels Data MT1-8

    Brush Engine MT1-8

  Hands-on Exercises MT1-9

    Exercise 1: Creating Marble Texture MT1-9

    Exercise 2: Creating Tileable Seamless Texture MT1-12

Exercise 3: Creating custom diffuse, bump, reflection, and displacement maps MT1-16

Exercise 4: Creating Door Mat Texture MT1-23

Exercise 5: Creating a Stripes Texture..MT1-27

Exercise 6: Creating Military Camouflage Texture MT1-28

Exercise 7: Creating Abstract Texture - I MT1-32

Exercise 8: Creating Digital Circuit Board Texture MT1-34

Exercise 9: Creating Leather Texture MT1-35

Exercise 10: Creating Lattice Wire Mesh Texture MT1-37

Exercise 11: Creating Brushed Metal Texture.....................................MT1-39

Example 12: Creating Reptile Skin Texture..MT1-40

Exercise 13 : Creating Sand Texture...MT1-42

Exercise 14: Creating Abstract Texture - II...MT1-45

Exercise 15: Creating an Organic Texture..MT1-48

Exercise 16: Creating Backgrounds - 1 ....MT1-51

Exercise 17: Creating Backgrounds - 2...MT1-53

Exercise 18: Creating Backgrounds - 3...MT1-56

Exercise 19: Creating Backgrounds - 4...MT1-57

Exercise 20: Creating Backgrounds - 5...MT1-58

Exercise 21: Creating Backgrounds - 6...MT1-60

Quiz **MT1-63**

Unit MT2 - Material Editors **MT2-1**

Compact Material Editor **MT2-1**

    Sample Slots **MT2-2**

    Hot and Cool Materials **MT2-2**

    Managing Materials with the Compact Material Editor.............**MT2-3**

Material/Map Browser **MT2-5**

Material Explorer **MT2-6**

Slate Material Editor MT2-6

   Selecting, Moving, and Laying Out Nodes.............................. MT2-9

   Previewing Materials MT2-10

   Wiring Nodes MT2-11

   Views MT2-12

Quiz MT2-14

Unit MT3 - Standard Materials and Maps MT3-1

General/Scanline Materials MT3-1

   Standard Material MT3-1

   Raytrace Material MT3-7

   Architectural Material MT3-7

   Advanced Lighting Override Material MT3-8

General Materials MT3-9

   Blend Material MT3-9

   Double Sided Material... MT3-9

   Composite Material MT3-9

   Morpher Material MT3-10

   Multi/Sub-Object Material MT3-10

   Shellac Material..MT3-11

   Top/Bottom Material MT3-11

   Matte/Shadow Material MT3-11

   Ink 'n Paint Material MT3-12

   DirectX Shader Material MT3-12

   XRef Material...MT3-12

   Physical Material MT3-12

General/Scanline Maps MT3-12

   Maps and Mapping Coordinates MT3-12

   UVW Mapping Coordinate Channels MT3-12

Real-World Mapping MT3-13

Output Rollout MT3-14

2D Maps MT3-15

3D Maps MT3-19

Compositor Maps MT3-21

Color Modifiers Maps MT3-21

Reflection and Refraction Maps MT3-22

Other Maps **MT3-22**

Shape Map MT3-22

Text Map MT3-22

TextureObjMask MT3-22

Color Map MT3-22

Combustion MT3-22

Map Output Selector MT3-23

MultiTile MT3-23

Hands-on Exercises **MT3-23**

Exercise 1: Creating the Gold Material MT3-23

Exercise 2: Creating the Copper Material MT3-25

Exercise 3: Creating the Brass Material MT3-26

Exercise 4: Creating the Chrome Material MT3-26

Exercise 5: Creating the Brushed Aluminum Material MT3-27

Exercise 6: Creating the Denim Fabric Material MT3-29

Exercise 7: Creating the Microscopic Material MT3-31

Exercise 8: Creating Material for a Volleyball MT3-32

Exercise 9: Creating Material for a Water Tunnel MT3-34

Exercise 10: Creating Rusted Metal Texture MT3-36

Exercise 11: Shading an outdoor Scene MT3-37

Exercise 12: Working with the ShapeMap MT3-40

Exercise 13: Working with Text Map MT3-42

Exercise 14: Working with TextureObjMask Map MT3-43

Quiz **MT3-44**

Unit MT4–Physical and Autodesk Materials. **MT4-1**

Autodesk Materials **MT4-1**

   Autodesk Ceramic **MT4-1**

   Autodesk Concrete **MT4-3**

   Autodesk Generic **MT4-4**

   Autodesk Glazing **MT4-4**

   Autodesk Harwood **MT4-4**

   Autodesk Masonry/CMU **MT4-5**

   Autodesk Metal **MT4-6**

   Autodesk Metallic Paint **MT4-6**

   Autodesk Mirror **MT4-6**

   Autodesk Plastic/Vinyl **MT4-6**

   Autodesk Solid Glass..**MT4-6**

   Autodesk Stone..**MT4-6**

   Autodesk Wall Paint **MT4-7**

   Autodesk Water **MT4-7**

Physical Material **MT4-7**

Hands-on Exercises **MT4-8**

   Exercise 1: Creating Glossy Varnished Wood MT4-8

   Exercise 2: Creating Glass Materials MT4-11

   Exercise 3: Creating Metal Materials...MT4-12

Quiz **MT4-14**

Unit ML1: Standard Lighting **ML1-1**

Standard Lights **ML1-1**

   Target Spotlight **ML1-2**

   Target Directional Light...**ML1-10**

Omni Light..ML1-11

Skylight ML1-11

Hands-On Exercises **ML1-12**

Exercise 1: Illuminating an Outdoor Scene ML1-12

Exercise 2: Quickly Rendering an Architectural Plan ML1-15

Exercise 3: Illuminating a Night Scene......................................ML1-18

Quiz **ML1-20**

Unit ML2: Photometric Lights **ML2-1**

Target Light...**ML2-1**

Template Rollout..ML2-2

General Parameters Rollout...ML2-3

Intensity/Color/Attenuation Rollout..................................ML2-4

Shape/Area Shadows Rollout...ML2-6

Distribution (Photometric File) Rollout ML2-7

Distribution (Spotlight) Rollout ML2-7

Free Light **ML2-7**

Quiz **ML2-8**

Unit ML3: Sunlight and Daylight Systems **ML3-1**

Using the Sunlight and Daylight Systems......................**ML3-1**

Daylight Parameters Rollout...ML3-2

Control Parameters Rollout ML3-3

Using Sun Positioner and Physical Sky **ML3-4**

Hands-on Exercise..**ML3-4**

Exercise 1: Shadow Pattern Study..ML3-4

Quiz **ML3-6**

Unit BT - Bonus Hands-on Exercises **BT-1**

Exercises - Texturing and Lighting **BT-1**

Exercise T1: Creating Balloon Material BT-1

Exercise T2: Creating Concrete Asphalt Material BT-2

Exercise T3: Creating Eyeball Material BT-3

Exercise T4: Creating Water Material BT-4

Exercise T5: Creating X-Ray Material BT-5

Exercise T6: Texturing a Cardboard Box BT-6

Exercise T7: Texturing a Dice BT-8

Appendix - A **AA1**

Index **I-1**

Other Books Published by Rising Polygon **OP-1**

This page is intentionally left blank

Acknowledgements

Thanks to:

Everyone at Autodesk [www.autodesk.com].
Everyone at Adobe [www.adobe.com].
Everyone at Microsoft [www.microsoft.com].

Thanks to all great digital artists who inspire us with their innovative VFX, gaming, animation, and motion graphics content.

And, a very special thanks to wonderful CG artists of London, UK.

Finally, thank you for picking up the book.

This page is intentionally left blank

About the Author

Rising Polygon, founded by **Ravi Conor** aka **ROC**, **Elizabeth VT**, and **Gordon Fisher** is a group of like-minded professionals and freelancers who are specialized in advertising, graphic design, web design and development, digital marketing, multimedia, exhibition, print design, branding, and CG content creation.

ROC has over a decade of experience in the computer graphics field and although he is primarily a shading and texturing artist, he is also experienced in the fields of Dynamics, UVMapping, Lighting, and Rendering. Along side CINEMA 4D, ROC has experience with VRay, Maya, FumeFX, Mudbox, 3ds Max, Mari, Photoshop, xNormal, UVLayout, Premiere, and After Effects.

Elizabeth is primarily an Android App developer. She is passionate about computer graphics and has an experience of over 6 years with 3ds Max, Maya, Photoshop, and Blender.

Gordon Fisher is the back bone of Rising Polygon and handles operations, finance, and accounts.

You can contact authors by sending an e-mail to the following Email ID: **raveeoc@gmail.com.**

This page is intentionally left blank

Preface

Why this Book?

The **3ds Max 2018 - Getting Started with Standard Materials and Lights** textbook offers a hands-on exercises based strategy for all those digital artists who have just started working on the 3ds Max [no experience needed] and interested in learning texturing and lighting in 3ds Max. This brilliant guide takes you step-by-step through the whole process of texturing, UV Mapping, and Lighting. From the very first pages, the users of the book will learn how to effectively use 3ds Max for shading and lighting surfaces.

The strength of this book is that it teaches all of the important concepts in an easy to understand language. As the readers move from hands-on exercise to hands-on exercise, they will be building their own portfolio of high quality artwork. One unit of the book presents a foundation of techniques to help you build custom textures, maps, and designs using Photoshop. Videos are provided for the hands-on exercises of this unit.

What you need?

To complete the examples and hands-on exercises in this book, you need 2018 version of Autodesk 3ds Max. Photoshop CC 2017 is used to create hands-on exercises of Unit MT1.

What are the main features of the book?
- The book is written using 3ds Max 2018 and Photoshop CC 2017 in an easy to understand language.
- Shading, texturing, lighting, and UV mapping techniques covered.
- 49 Hands-on exercises to hone your skills.
- Detailed coverage of tools and features.
- Additional tips, guidance, and advice is provided.
- Important terms are in bold face so that you never miss them.
- Support for technical aspect of the book.
- 3ds Max files and PSDs/textures used are available for download from the accompanying website.
- You will also get access to a ePub file that has the **color images** of the screenshots/ diagrams used in this book. These images will help you to understand the HOEs and output. The ePub file is included with the resources.

How This Book Is Structured?
This book is divided into following units:

Unit MT1 - Creating Textures in Photoshop

- Understanding non-destructive editing
- Creating custom textures and designs
- Creating maps

Unit MT2 - Material Editors

- **Compact Material Editor**
- **Slate Material Editor**

Unit MT3 - Standard Materials and Maps

- General/Scanline materials
- General maps

Unit MT4 - Physical and Autodesk Materials

- Autodesk Materials
- Physical Material

Unit ML1 - Standard Lights

- Basic Lighting Concepts
- Creating and placing lights
- 3ds Max Lights
- Light Linking
- Shadows
- Lighting Effects

Unit ML2 - Photometric Lights

- Photometric light types: **Target Light**, and **Free Light**
- Color temperatures
- Shadow generating shapes
- Exposure controls

Unit ML3 - Sunlight and Daylight Systems

- Sunlight and Daylight Systems
- Positioning the Compass
- Choosing a location
- Sun Positioner and Physical Sky

Unit MBT - Bonus hands-on Exercises

Examination Copies

Books received as examination copies are for review purposes only and may not be made available for student use. Resale of the examination copies is prohibited. If you want to receive this book as an examination copy, send the request from your official e-mail id to us using the **Contact** page from our website.

Electronic Files

Any electronic file associated with this book are licensed to the original user only. These files can not be transferred to a third party. However, the original user can use these files in personal projects without taking any permission from **Rising Polygon**.

Trademarks

CINEMA 4D is the registered trademarks of **Maxon Computers**. **Windows** is the registered trademarks of **Microsoft Inc**. **3ds Max** is the registered trademarks of **Autodesk Inc**.

Disclaimer

Access to Electronic Files

This book is sold via multiple sales channels. If you don't have access to the resources used in this book, you can place a request for the resources by visiting the following link: *http://bit.ly/resources-rp.*

Customer Support

At **Rising Polygon**, our technical team is always ready to take care of your technical queries. If you are facing any problem with the technical aspect of the book, navigate to *http://bit.ly/contact-rp* and let us know about your query.

Reader Feedback

Your feedback is always welcome. Your feedback is critical to our efforts at **Rising Polygon** and it will help us in developing quality titles in the future. To send the feedback, visit *http://bit.ly/contact-rp*.

Errata

We take every precaution while preparing the content of the book but mistakes do happen. If you find any mistake in this book general or technical, we would be happy that you report it to us so that we can mention it in the errata section of the book's online page. If you find any errata, please report them by visiting the following link: *http://bit.ly/contact-rp*. This will help the other readers from frustration. Once your errata is verified, it will appear in the errata section of the book's online page.

Contact Author

Stay connected with us through Twitter (**@risingpolygon**) to know the latest updates about our products, information about books, and other related information. You can also send an e-mail to author at the following address: **raveeoc@gmail.com**.

Unit MT1 - Creating Textures in Photoshop

Photoshop provides intuitive and cutting-edge image editing features. These features improve your efficiency and artwork as you incorporate them into your workflow. In this section, I am discussing some techniques, tips, and concepts that will help you in creating some cool textures and background designs. These techniques will help you in creating cool looking backgrounds and textures for your 3ds Max scenes.

In this unit, I will describe the following:

- Understanding non-destructive editing
- Creating custom textures and designs
- Creating custom diffuse, specular, bump, reflection, and normal maps

Non-destructive Editing

Photoshop offers non-destructive editing features. This is the one of the reasons that it remains an essential part of a texturing artist's and designer's toolset. Non-destructive editing allows you to make changes to an image without changing pixel data in the original image. There are many ways in Photoshop that enable you to perform non-destructive editing. Here, I will discuss only those techniques/concepts that are useful for texturing artists/designers.

Adjustment Layers

The **Adjustment** layers non-destructively alter underlying tones and colors [see Figure F1]. These layers apply color and tonal adjustments to the image without changing the pixel data. The adjustments are stored in the adjustment layer and applied to the all layers below it. On the other hand, the fill layers fill a layer with color, gradient, or pattern and do not affect the layers underneath.

F1

Tip: Clipping Adjustment Layers
*You can clip an adjustment layer to affect only one layer in the **Layers** panel. To clip a layer, hold*
***Alt** and move the mouse pointer on the boundary of the two layers. When the shape of the pointer*
changes, click to enable layer clipping.

The other advantages of using the adjustment layers are as follows:

- You can re-edit the adjustment layer any time.
- You can tone down the adjustment layer's effect by lowering the opacity of the layer.
- You can reset the effect of the layer.
- You can perform selective editing by using the adjustment layer's mask.
- You can apply adjustments to the multiple documents by copying and pasting adjustment layers between documents.
- You can adjust the blending mode to merge their effect with other layers.
- You can toggle their visibility on and off to preview the before and after comparisons.
- You can rearrange, delete, hide, and duplicate the adjustment layers.

Filtering with Smart Filter

Any filter that you apply to a smart object is a smart filter. These filters appear below the smart objects in the **Layers** panel. If you select a layer and then choose **Convert for Smart Filters** from the **Filter** menu, the selected layer is converted to a smart object and then you can apply smart filters onto the smart object [see Figure F2].

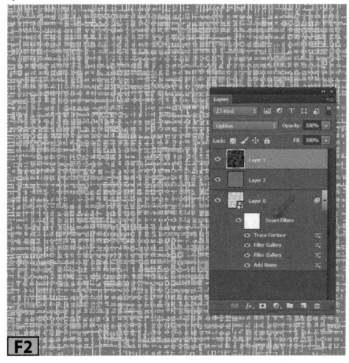

Note: Smart Filters

Note: Smart Filters

You can use any Photoshop filter as smart filter except **Extract**, **Liquify**, **Pattern Maker**, and **Vanishing Point**.

Like the **Adjustment** layers, you can re-edit smart filters, change their order, blending mode, and so forth. To expand or collapse the view of the **Smart Filters**, click the triangle next to the **Smart Filter** icon. If you want to expand the new effects by default, choose **Panel Options** from the **Layers** panel. On the **Layers Panel Options** dialog that appears [see Figure F3], check the **Expand New Effects** check box.

Tip: Smart Filters

You can apply the **Shadow/Highlight** and **Variations** commands as **Smart Filters**.

Note: Gallery

If you apply more than one filter using **Filter Gallery**, they appear as a group with the name **Filter Gallery**.

Retouching on a Separate Layer

Clone Stamp Tool (also referred to as **Clone Tool**) is extensively used by the texturing artists to retouch the textures. This tool and other retouching tools such as **Healing Brush**, and **Spot Healing Brush** tools let you retouch non-destructively on a separate layer.

When you are retouching on a separate layer, make sure that **All Layers** is selected from the **Sample** drop-down in the options bar [see Figure F4].

Figures F5 and F6 show the original texture and randomize texture created using **Clone Stamp Tool**, respectively.

Tip: Ignoring Adjustment Layers

Click the **Ignore Adjustment Layers** button to ensure that you won't sample from the adjustment layers. This button is available on the right of the **Sample** drop-down [see Figure F4].

Tip: Clone Stamp Tool
*If you use the default round brushes with the **Clone Stamp Tool**, you will get soft and blurred clones.
To get rid of this behavior, use a custom shaped grungy brush.*

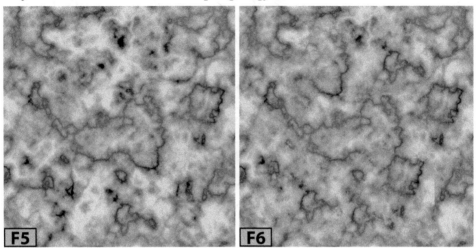

F5   F6

Nondestructive Crop

After you create the crop rectangle using the **Crop** tool, ensure that **Delete Cropped Pixels** is turned off on the **Crop Tool** options bar [see Figure F7] and then crop the image. To restore the cropped data anytime, choose **Reveal All** from the **Image** menu.

F7

Tip: Crop Tool
*You can also reveal pixels by dragging **Crop Tool** beyond the edges of an image.*

Masking

Masks in Photoshop are used to hide portions of a layer or reveal the portions of the layers below [see Figure F8]. The masks are non-destructive, you can re-edit them any time. As discussed earlier, the **Filter** masks allows you to mask out the effect of the **Smart Filters**.

Tip: Adding layer mask to the Background layer
*If you want to apply a layer mask to a **Background** layer, you need to first convert it to regular layer by choosing, **New | Layer from Background** from the **Layer** menu.*

Blending Modes

Blending modes control how a layer blends with the pixels in the layers beneath it [see Figure F9]. You can use the blending modes to generate various effects that you can use to create cool textures, especially organic textures. The **Overlay**, **Multiply**, and **Soft Light** modes in particular are very useful and extensively used by the texturing artists. **Blending** modes in **Photoshop** are grouped category wise.

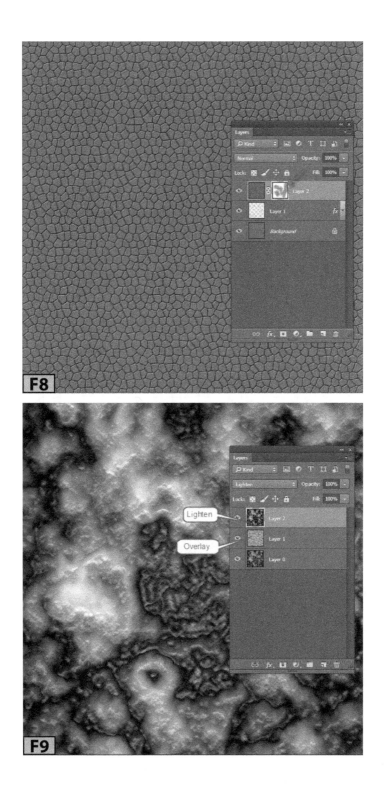

Here's is a quick rundown:

Normal Category
The members of this category are **Normal,** and **Dissolve**. The resulting color of the pixels is not affected by the color of underlying pixels unless **Opacity** of the source layer is not less than **100%**.

Subtractive Category
The members of this category are **Darken, Multiply, Color Burn, Linear Burn,** and **Darker Color**. These modes tend to darken the colors.

Additive Category
The members of this category are **Lighten, Screen, Color Dodge, Linear Dodge (Add),** and **Lighter Color**. These modes tend to lighten the colors.

Complex Category
The members of this category are **Overlay, Soft Light, Hard Light, Linear Light, Vivid Light, Pin Light,** and **Hard Mix**. These modes perform different operations on the layers. The result depends on whether one of the colors is lighter than **50%** gray.

Difference Category
The members of this category are **Difference, Exclusion, Subtract,** and **Divide**. These modes generate the final color based on the differences between the values of the source color and underlying color.

HSL Category
The members of this category are **Hue, Saturation, Color,** and **Luminosity**. These modes transfer one or more of the components (hue, saturation, and luminosity) from the underlying color to the result color.

Specifying a Tonal Range for Blending Layers
The **Blend If** sliders available in the **Blending Options** section of the **Layer Style** dialog [see Figure F10] give you ability to control which pixels from the active layer and the underlying layers appear in the final image.

You can remove dark pixels from the active layer or make the bright pixels visible from the underlying layer. You can also blend the pixels to create a smooth transition. You can also specify which channel data you want to blend, the default is **Gray** which specifies the blending range for all channels [see Figure F10].

Tip: Defining a range of partially blended pixels
*To define a range of partially blended pixels, hold **Alt** and then drag the one of a slider triangle [see Figure given next].*

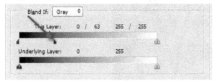

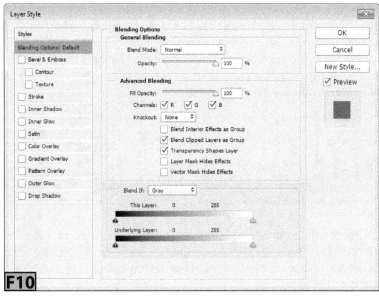

F10

High Pass Filter

This filter, that you can access from **Other** sub-menu of the **Filter** menu, is useful for sharpening the image as well as for creating a base image for the bump maps. For enhancing the images, create a copy of the layer, and then apply the **High Pass** filter to it with a relatively low radius. Now, blend the two layers using the **Overlay** blending mode.

Note: High Pass Filter
*This filter produces an effect opposite to that of the **Gaussian Blur** filter. This filter is also useful for extracting line art.*

To get the base image for the bump map, apply the **High Pass** filter with relatively high radius value to the image [see Figure F11].

F11

Using Channels Data

You can use the channel data to quickly create base images for bump and reflection maps. To create base image for bump or reflection map, you can use the red and blue channels, respectively [see Figure F12]. To create base images, select the red or blue channel from the **Channels** panel and then press **Ctrl+A** to select all channel data. Create a new document and press **Ctrl+V** to paste the data. Now, you can use the **Levels** adjustment to create bump or reflection map.

F12

Brush Engine

The **Brush Engine** in Photoshop is robust and extremely powerful. You can create brushes that apply paint to images in a variety of ways. You can select an existing preset brush, or create a unique brush tip from part of an image. Creating brushes from any image is extremely easy, make a selection and then choose **Define Brush Preset** from the **Edit** menu.

The **Brush** panel [see Figure F13] not only allows you to select preset brushes but also lets you modify (add enhancement) the existing brushes and design new custom brushes.

F13

There are many options in the **Brush** panel that you can use to add enhancements to your brush. Among the most useful are **Shape Dynamics**, **Scattering**, and **Smoothing**.

When you use brush for painting on your textures, it is recommended that you use a build-up approach. Always start with low opacity brush settings and then build up the tone slowly. The end result will depend on how efficiently you have used the opacity settings.

Hands-on Exercises

Before you start the hands-on exercises, let's first create a project folder that will host the exercise files. Navigate to the folder where you want to save the files and then create a new folder with the name **unit-mt1**.

Exercise 1: Creating Marble Texture

Let's start with creating a marble texture [see Figure E1] using filters and image adjustment commands. In the process, you will learn about equalizing images in Photoshop. Before tiling your textures, you need to fix problems such as uneven brightness, visible seams, and shift in colors.

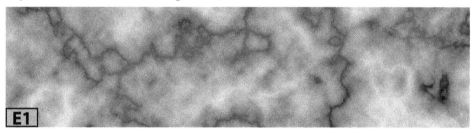

E1

The following table summarizes the exercise:

Table E1: Creating the Marble Texture	
Skill level	Intermediate
Time to complete	15 Minutes
Project Folder	**unit-mt1**
Final exercise file	**umt1-hoe-1.psd**
Video	**UMT1VID-HOE-1.MP4**

Open **Photoshop** and create a **1000x1000** px document. Save the document with the name **umt1-hoe-1.psd**. Unlock the **Background** layer and then press **D** to set the black and white colors for the foreground and background, respectively. Choose **Render | Difference Cloud** from the **Filter** menu to apply the filter on the **Layer 0** layer [see Figure E2].

Note: Difference Cloud Filter

*The **Difference Clouds** filter randomly generates values between the foreground and background colors to create a cloud pattern. This filter blends the colors in the same way the **Difference** mode blends. The first time you apply this filter, a cloud pattern is created by Photoshop. If you apply this filter a subsequent number of times, ribs and veins are created that resembles a marble texture.*

Repeatedly apply the **Difference Clouds** filter until you get the basic marble texture you are looking for [see Figure E3]. Duplicate **Layer 0** and rename it as **Layer 1**. Choose **Blur | Average** from the **Filter** menu to apply filter to **Layer 1** [see Figure E4].

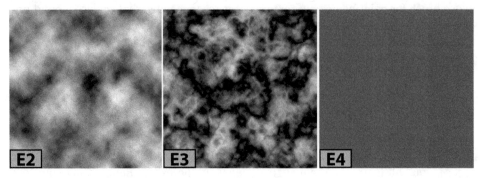

E2　**E3**　**E4**

The **Average** filter averages color of an image or selection and then fill the image or selection with that color. It helps in creating smooth looking textures.

Warning: Transparent Pixels
Unexpected results are produced if you average pixels from the transparent regions.

Place **Layer 1** underneath **Layer 0** in the **Layers** panel. Set the **Blending Mode** of **Layer 0** to **Linear Light** and then set **Opacity** to **50%**. Make sure **Layer 0** is selected and then choose **Other | High Pass** from the **Filter** menu. In the **High Pass** dialog that appears, set **Radius** to **120** and click **OK** [refer to Figure E5].

The **High Pass** filter allows you to retain the edge details in the specified radius where sharp color transitions occur in the image. It then suppresses the rest of the image.

Note: High Pass Filter
*The **High Pass** filter creates a smooth version of the image. For example, if you apply this filter to a grass texture, it will convert the image to a homogeneous patch of green [see the image on the right].*

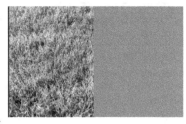

Note: High Pass Filter
*This filter produces the opposite effect that of the **Gaussian Blur** filter.*

Tip: Extracting Line Art
This filter is useful in extracting line art and large black and white areas from the scanned images.

Choose **Adjustments | Shadows/Highlight** from the **Image** menu. In the **Shadows/Highlight** dialog that appears, set **Amount** to **100** in the **Shadows** group. Make sure **Amount** in the **Highlights** group is set to **0** and then click **OK** [see Figure E6].

The **Shadows/Highlights** command lightens or darkens the image based on the surrounding pixels. The default values in the **Shadows/Highlights** dialog are meant for fixing images having backlight problem.

Note: Shadows/Highlights Command
You can also use this command to correct washed out images because they were close to the camera flash.

Choose **Adjustments | Color Balance** from the **Image** menu. In the **Color Balance** dialog that appears, set the values as shown in Figure E7 and then click **OK**.

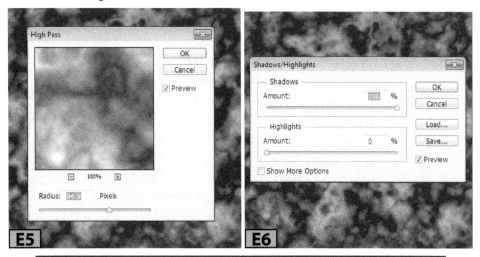

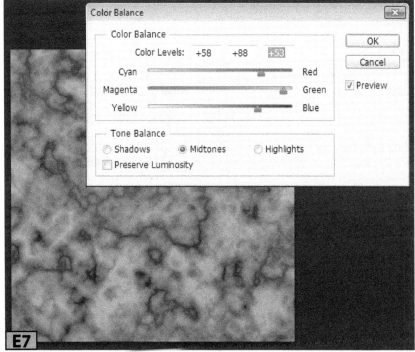

The **Color Balance** command allows you to change the overall mix of the colors in the image. You can use this command for a generalized color correction. Press **Ctrl+E** to merge the layers. Choose **Adjustments | Exposure** from the **Image** menu. In the **Exposure** dialog that appears, set **Exposure** to **0.65** and **Offset** to **-0.0244**. Press **Ctrl+S** to save the document.

Tip: Equalize Command

You can also use the **Equalize** command from the **Image | Adjustment** menu. The **Equalize** command redistributes the brightness values so that they represent entire range of the brightness values.

Tip: Hue/Saturation command

Use the **Hue/Saturation** command if you want to change the color of the marble.

Note: Exposure Command

The **Exposure** command is primarily used with HDR images. It adjusts tonality of the image in the **Linear** color space.

Exercise 2: Creating Tileable Seamless Texture

Here, you will learn to create a tileable seamless texture in Photoshop [see Figure E1]. This technique is very useful and often used by texturing/digital artists if they have to repeat a texture or pattern. In this example, you will use the **Offset** filter and some Photoshop techniques.

The following table summarizes the exercise:

Table E2: Creating Tileable Seamless Texture	
Skill level	Intermediate
Time to complete	45 Minutes
Project Folder	**unit-mt1**
Final exercise file	**umt1-hoe-2.psd**
Video	**UMT1VID-HOE-2.MP4**

Launch **Photoshop** and then open **grungeMetal.jpg**. In order to create a tileable texture, first you will make the texture [that you want to make seamless] square. Pick the **Crop** tool from **Tool Box** and then RMB click on the canvas, choose **1x1 [Square]** from the popup menu that appears [see Figure E2]. Press **Enter** to commit the changes.

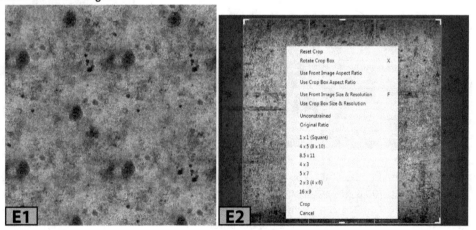

The **Crop** tool allows you to remove unwanted portions of an image. It also gives you ability to straighten the images. The **Crop** tool is non-destructive tool meaning you can retain the cropped pixels to optimize the crop boundaries later. When you perform a crop on an image, Photoshop gives you real-time feedback to visualize the final result.

Choose **Image Size** from the **Image** menu. In the **Image Size** dialog that appears, set **Width** and **Height** to **496** and then click **OK**. Save the Photoshop document as **umt1-hoe-2.psd**.

Tip: Document Size
*The reason we have changed size from **497** to **496** is that we want an even number [divisible by **2**] here because the **Offset** filter that we will apply later does not accept decimal values.*

Now, let's get rid of the lines or scratches from the texture [see left image in Figure E3]. The reason we want to get rid of those scratches is that they might look odd when texture is tiled. Pick **Clone Stamp Tool** from **Tool Box**. Choose a noise brush [see Figure E4] for **Clone Stamp Tool** and then get rid of those scratches [see right image in Figure E3].

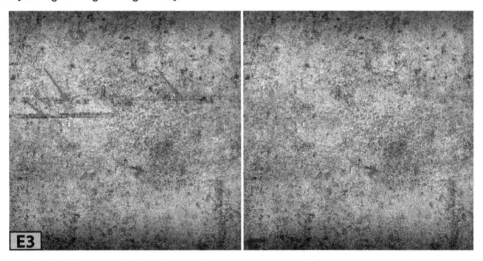

Clone Stamp Tool allows you to duplicate objects or remove a defect in an image. You can use this tool to paint one part of an image to another part of the same image or over another part. You can also paint contents of one layer to another layer. This tool also allows you to set a brush tip.

Now, let's add some more details to the texture. Open **oilTexture.jpg** and place it on the **umt1-hoe-2.psd's** canvas [see Figure E5]. Set **Blending Mode** to **Multiply** for the oil texture.

Add a **Levels** adjustment layer and clip it to the oil texture layer. Adjust the levels [see Figure E6]. Ensure the oil texture layer is selected and then click the **Add layer mask** from the **Layers** panel.

Set the foreground color to black and pick a noise brush. Now, paint black on the mask to get rid of the seams and unwanted area [see Figure E7].

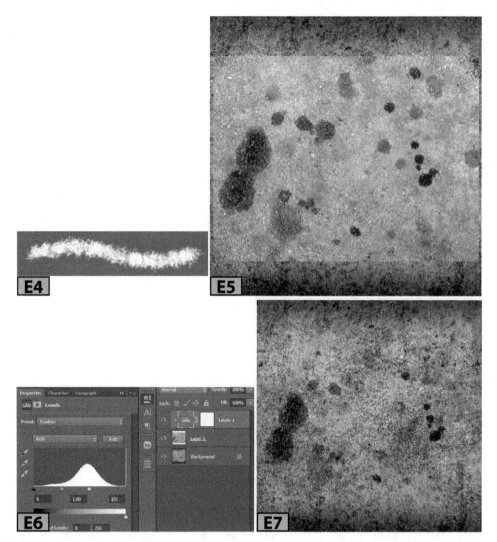

Press **Ctrl+A** to select all pixels and then choose **Copy Merged** from the **Image** menu. Press **Ctrl+V** to paste the data. Ensure the layer is at the top of the stack in the **Layers** panel. Rename layer as **Base**. Press **Ctrl+J** to duplicate the layer and then rename the layer as **Base1**. Choose **Other | Offset** from the **Filter** menu. In the **Offset** dialog that appears, set the parameters as shown in Figure E8 and then click **OK** [see Figure E9].

Note: Offset Command
*We have used the value **248** pixels for **Horizontal** and **Vertical** because it's half the value of **496**, the **50%** of the original size.*

The **Wrap Around** feature fills the undefined space with content from the opposite edge of the image.

Ensure the **Base1** layer is selected in the **Layers** panel. Click the **Add layer mask** button to add a layer mask. Ensure the **Foreground Color** is set to **Black** and then pick a noise brush. Using the **Brush** tool, paint on the seams to get rid of them.

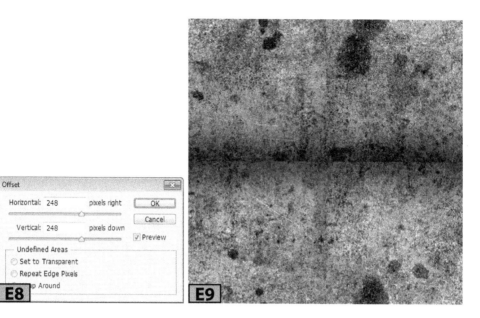

When you paint black, you reveal the layer underneath [see Figure E10].

Tip: Adding randomness to the texture
Paint on some other areas [not just the seams] to get some randomness in the texture.

Tip: Adding randomness
*You can add more randomness by cloning the some area using **Clone Stamp Tool**. You can also use **Healing Brush Tool** to clone some areas. This tool allows you to preserve the luminosity of the pixels.*

Choose **Flatten Image** from the **Layer** menu and then unlock the **Background** layer. Choose **Canvas Size** from the **Image** menu. In the **New Size** section of the **Canvas Size** dialog that appears, set the values as shown in Figure E11 and click **OK**.

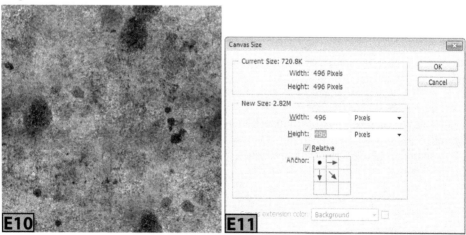

Pick **Move Tool** from the **Tool Box** and then **Alt+drag** layer on the canvas. Press **Shift** to snap the movement [see Figure E12]. Similarly, create two more copies [see Figure E13]. Select all layers in the **Layers** panel and press **Ctrl+E** to merge all layers.

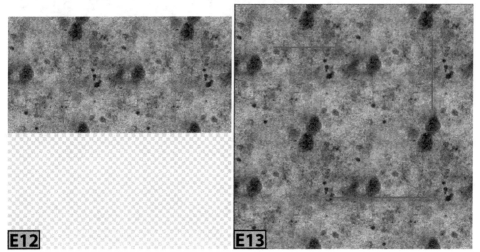

Tip: Order of the layers
Create and place layers in clockwise direction [see Figure E13].

Note: Flatten Image
The **Flatten Image** *command reduces the file size by merging all visible layers. Any remaining transparent area is filled with white.*

Warning: Flatten Image
When you use this command, the images are merged permanently. You cannot revert to the unflattened state.

Warning: Flatten Image
Photoshop also flatten the images, if you switch between the color modes. Therefore, I recommend that you make a backup of your document before switching the color modes.

If you find some seams in the image or if you want to break the symmetry do not hesitate in using **Clone Stamp Tool**.

Exercise 3: Creating custom diffuse, bump, reflection, and displacement maps

This exercise deals with creating custom diffuse, bump, reflection, and displacement maps that you can use in any 3D application of your choice. In this exercise, you will first create the diffuse map by converting an image to a seamless texture and then you will use various techniques to create other maps from the seamless diffuse map.

The following table summarizes the exercise:

Table E3: Creating custom diffuse, bump, reflection, and displacement maps	
Skill level	Intermediate
Time to complete	60 Minutes
Project Folder	**unit-mt1**
Video	**UMT1VID-HOE-3.MP4**

Open Photoshop. Create a **2000x2000** px document. Save the file as **concreteBare_Diffuse.psd**. Open **Concrete_L.jpg** and drag it to **concreteBare_Diffuse.psd** Photoshop file. Now, place **Concrete_L.jpg** as shown in Figure E1. Rename the layer as **Base** [see Figure E2].

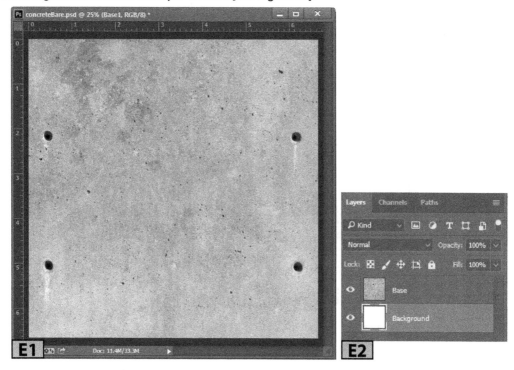

From the **Filter** menu, choose **Other | Offset** to open the **Offset** dialog. In this dialog, set **Horizontal** and **Vertical** to **1000**. Also, make sure **Wrap Around** is chosen in the **Undefined Areas** group.

You will see that the offset is not centered on the canvas even if I have set **Horizontal** and **Vertical** to **1000** units which is half the size of the document. It happens because **Offset** filter takes whole image into account not just the visible area of the canvas [see Figure E3]. Choose **Cancel** from the **Offset** dialog. To overcome this issue, I will select the visible area of the image and then apply the **Offset** filter.

Press **Ctrl+A** to select the visible area of the image and then press **Ctrl+J** to create a layer from the selection. Rename the new layer as **Base1**. From the **Filter** menu, choose **Other | Offset** to open the **Offset** dialog. In this dialog, set **Horizontal** and **Vertical** to **1000** and then click **OK** to offset the texture [see Figure E4].

Create a copy of **Base** and then move it above **Base1** [see Figure E5]. Add a layer mask to the **Base copy** and fill it with **black** [see Figure E6]. Set **white** as active color and then make sure the layer mask is selected. Now, use a grunge or noise brush and paint on the seams using white color [see Figure E7].

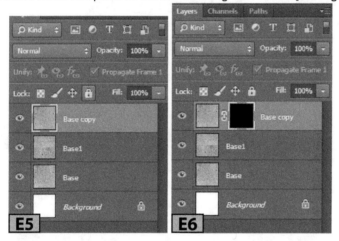

Now, choose a different noise brush and randomly paint to reveal some more texture. Choose **Flatten Image** from the **Layer** menu to collapse all layers. Create clones of holes on their opposite side using **Clone Stamp** tool [see Figure E8].

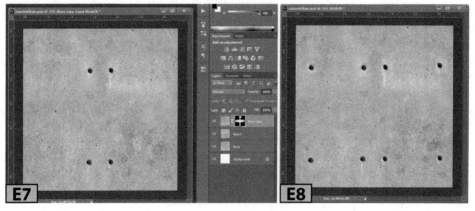

Now, add a **Levels** adjustment layer and adjust the levels [see Figure E9]. Make sure the layer mask of **Level 1** layer is selected. Now, paint black to get the some of the details back from the state prior to applying levels [see Figure E10].

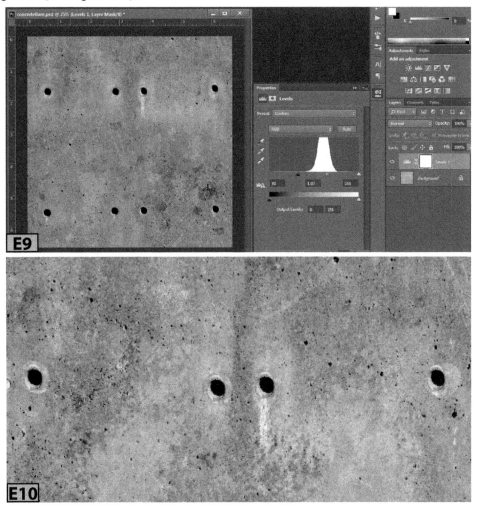

Note: Levels Command
*The **Levels** command/adjustment layer allows you to make adjustment to the tonal range and color balance of an image. This command adjusts the intensity levels of shadows, midtones, and highlights of an image. The histogram that this command provides, gives you a visual feed for adjusting the key tones of the image [see the image on the right].*

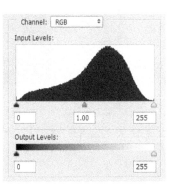

Tip: Correcting Exposure and Color Balance
*You can quickly fix issues like color balance and incorrect exposure using the **Levels** command. The shortcut key to invoke this command is **Ctrl+L**.*

Open **Grunge_A.jpg** and place it on the **concreteBare_Diffuse.psd** image. Open the **Layer Style** dialog and adjust the **Blend If** options as shown in Figure E11 and then click **OK**. Add a layer mask to the grunge layer and make sure it is selected. Now, paint with black color using a noise brush to get rid of the seams [see Figure E12]. Save the Photoshop file.

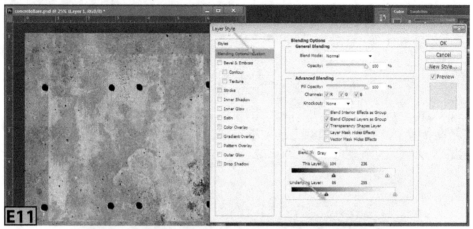

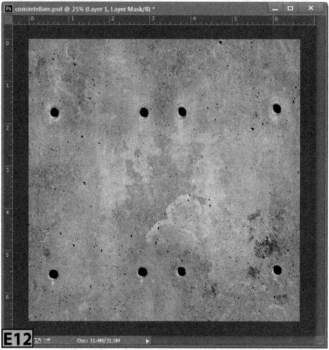

Tip: Adding Contrast to the Image
*If any image does not use the full tonal range, you can use the **Shadow** and **Highlight** input sliders inward until they touch the end of histogram. See the before and after images given next.*

 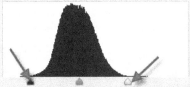

Next, you will create the reflection map. You can create this map by desaturating the image [Shortcut: **Shift+Ctrl+U**] and then using levels to exaggerate contrast in the image. However, I like to use the blue channel of the image to create reflection map as this channel already has some contrast by default. Let's do it.

Note: The Desaturate Command
*The **Desaturate** command is responsible for converting color values to the grayscale values. However, it does not change the color mode of the image. This command produces results similar to that of the **Hue/Saturation** command when you set **Saturation** to -100.*

Warning: The Desaturate Command
*If you are working with a multi-layer document, the **Desaturate** command converts the selected layer to grayscale values.*

On the **Channels** panel, click the **Blue** layer. Press **Ctrl+A** and then **Shift+Ctrl+C** to copy the information. Now, create a new **Photoshop** document and press **Ctrl+V** to paste the data. **Shift+Ctrl+C** is the shortcut key for the **Copy Merged** command. This command copies merged data of all visible layers in the selected area. In contrast, the **Copy** command copies the selected area on the active layer. Add a **Levels** adjustment layer and exaggerate contrast in the image [see Figure E13]. Save the file as **concreteBare_Reflection.psd**.

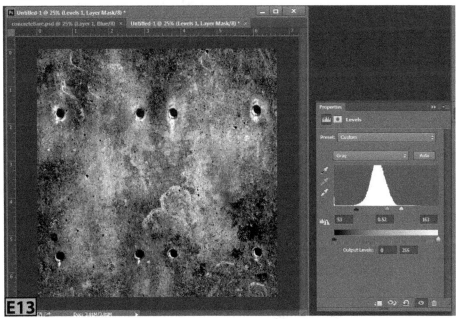

Similarly, to create the bump map, use the red channel information and adjust levels to lighten the tone [see Figure E14]. If you want more details, you can use the **Brightness and Contrast** adjustment to boost the contrast [see Figure E15]. Save the file as **concreteBare_Bump.psd**.

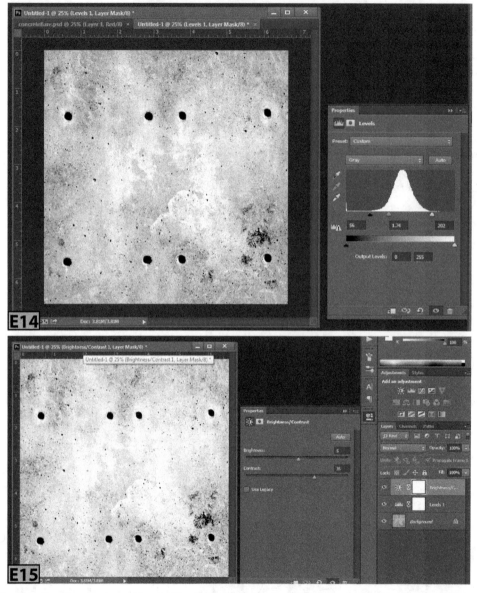

To create the displacement map, copy the bump map and paste it in a new document. Add a **Levels** adjustment layer and adjust levels until you get the cleaner holes [see Figure E16]. Keep in mind that the white area will be displaced on rendering, the black area will be left alone.

Now, blur the image with the **Gaussian Blur** filter with the strength of **1.3** for smooth displacement map. Save the file as **concreteBare_Displacement.psd**.

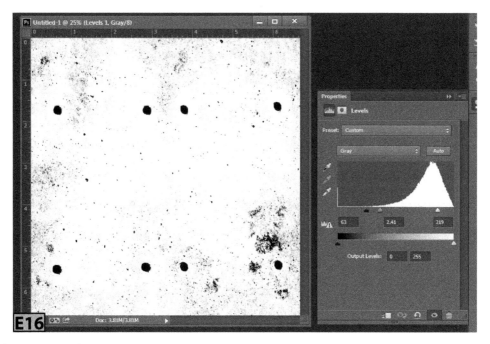

E16

Exercise 4: Creating Door Mat Texture

In this example, you will create a doormat texture [see Figure E1]. You can use the same technique to create various types of fabrics and special effects. The following table summarizes the exercise:

Table E4: Creating Door Mat Texture	
Skill level	Basic
Time to complete	15 Minutes
Project Folder	**unit-mt1**
Final exercise file	**umt1-hoe-4.psd**
Video	**UMT1VID-HOE-4.MP4**

Open Photoshop and create a **960x540px** document. Save the document with the name **umt1-hoe-4.psd**. Fill the document with **50%** gray using the **Edit | Fill** command. Choose **Noise | Add Noise** from the **Filter** menu and then set the parameters, as shown in Figure E2. Click **OK**.

E1

E2

Note: Add Noise Filter

*The **Add Noise** filter applies random pixels to an image. You can use this filter in a variety of ways. From reducing banding from the feathered selections to give realistic looks to the heavily retouched areas, from making a texture realistic to creating special effects.*

*It provides two options for noise distribution: **Uniform** and **Gaussian**. The **Uniform** method creates a subtle effect whereas the **Gaussian** method produces a speckled effect. You can use the **Monochromatic** option if you just want to affect the tonal values leaving the color unchanged.*

Choose **Blur | Gaussian Blur** from the **Filter** menu and then set **Radius** to **1** in the **Gaussian Blur** dialog that appears. Click **OK**. Choose **Stylize | Wind** from the **Filter** menu and then select **Stagger** from the **Method** section. Select **From the Left** from the **Direction** section [see Figure E3]. Click **OK**.

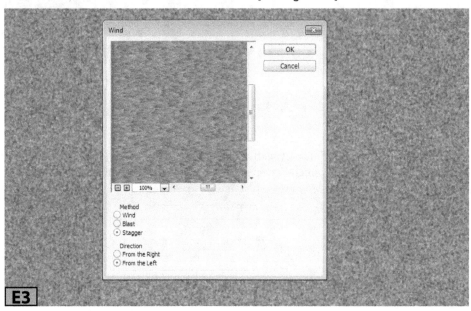

Note: Wind Filter

*The **Wind** filter applies tiny lines to the image simulating a windblown effect. It has three types: **Wind**, **Blast**, and **Stagger**. The **Stagger** is more dramatic than the other two methods. This method offsets lines in the image [see the imaged below].*

Unlock the **Background** layer and apply the **Color Overlay** style to it [see Figure E4]. Use the following color: **#964605**.

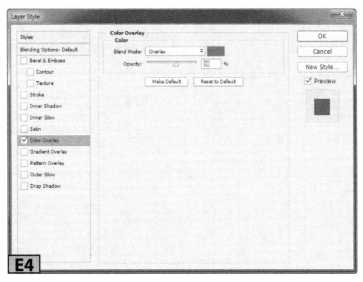

E4

Pick **Crop Tool** from **Tool Box** and then RMB click on the canvas, choose **1x1 [Square]** from the popup menu that appears. Press **Enter** to commit the changes [see Figure E5]. Now, if you check the size of the image, it should be **540x540px**. Notice in Figure E5, the fiber strands not oriented correctly. We need to change their orientation to vertical. Let's do it.

Note: High-res Seamless Texture
Use the technique explained in Exercise 1 to create a high-res seamless texture.

Choose **Image Rotation | 90 Counter Clockwise** from the **Image** menu to change the orientation of the strands [see Figure E6]. Now, let's add some text [**Welcome**] on the texture and apply some styling to it. Pick **Horizontal Type Tool** from **Tool Box** and type **"Welcome"** using a font of your choice. Set **Fill** to **0%** for the **Welcome** layer.

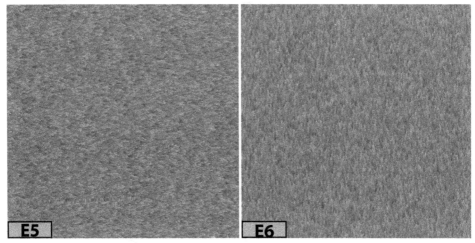

E5   **E6**

Tip: Wide Fonts
Wider fonts will appear good on this texture.

Apply the **Inner Shadow** layer style to the **Welcome** layer [see Figure E7]. Now, apply the **Stroke** layer style [see Figure E8]. Press **Ctrl+S** to save the file. Figure E1 shows the end result.

E7

E8

Exercise 5: Creating a Stripes Texture

In this example, you will create stripes as shown in Figure E1.

The following table summarizes the exercise:

Table E5: Creating a Stripes Texture	
Skill level	Basic
Time to complete	15 Minutes
Project Folder	**unit-mt1**
Final exercise file	**umt1-hoe-5.psd**
Video	**UMT1VID-HOE-5.MP4**

Create a new **1000x1000 px** Photoshop document and then set the **Foreground** and **Background** colors as follows: **#995a00** and **#dcab4c**. Choose **Render | Difference Clouds** from the **Filter** menu [see Figure E2]. Choose **Filter Gallery | Texture | Patchwork** from the **Filter** menu and then set **Square Size** to **5** and **Relief** to **25**. Click **OK** [see Figure E3].

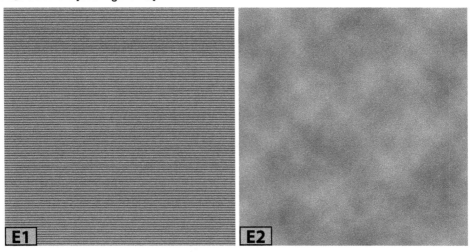

Note: Patchwork Filter
It breaks the image into squares. These squares are filled with the predominant color in that area of the image. It randomly reduces or increases the tile depth to make highlights and shadows.

Choose **Blur | Motion Blur** from the **Filter** menu. In the **Motion Blur** dialog that opens, set **Angle** to **0, Distance** to **2000** and then click **OK** [see Figure E4]. Save the document with the name **umt1-hoe-5.psd**.

Note: Motion Blur Filter
This filter is used to blur pixels in the specified direction. You can specify the range from –360 degrees to +360 degrees. The range for motion blur intensity is from 1 to 999.

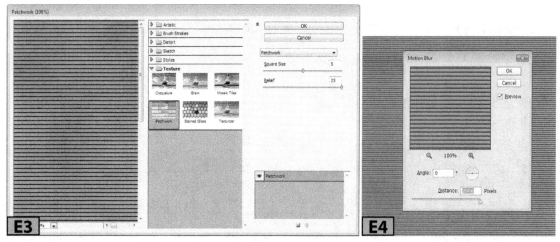

Exercise 6: Creating Military Camouflage Texture

In this example, you will create a green camouflage texture using various filters [see Figure E1]. The following table summarizes the exercise:

Table E3: Creating Military Camouflage Texture	
Skill level	Basic
Time to complete	20 Minutes
Project Folder	**unit-mt1**
Final exercise file	**umt1-hoe-6.psd**
Video	**UMT1VID-HOE-6.MP4**

Open **Photoshop** and create a **1000x1000** px document. Save the document with the name **umt1-hoe-3. psd**. Fill the document with the color: **#394f25**. Choose **Filter Gallery | Texture | Texturizer** from the **Filter** menu and then use the settings shown in Figure E2. Figure E3 shows the texture.

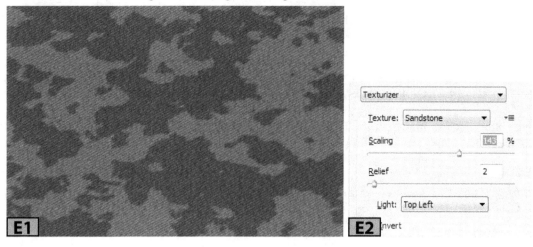

The **Texturizer** *filter applies a texture to the image. It has four built-in textures:* **Brick**, **Burlap**, **Canvas**, *and* **Standalone** *[see the imaged below].*

You can also load your custom texture by using the drop-down located next to the **Texture** *parameter [refer Figure E2]. The* **Light** *parameter can be used to change the direction of the light. Figure on the right shows the* **Brick** *texture with* **Light** *set to* **Bottom Right**.

Unlock the **Background** layer and then create a copy of it. Rename the new layer as **Layer 1**. Choose **Filter Gallery | Sketch | Water Paper** from the **Filter** menu and then use the settings shown in Figure E4. Set the **Blending Mode** to **Linear Light** and **Opacity** to **24%**. Figure E5 shows the texture.

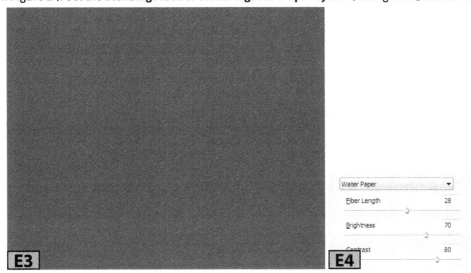

Note: Water Paper Filter

The **Water Paper** *filter produces blotchy daub that appears to be carelessly painted on a damp paper.*

Duplicate **Layer 0** and rename it as **Layer 2**. Move it to the top of the stack. Choose **Filter Gallery | Sketch | Halftone Pattern** from the **Filter** menu and then use the settings shown in Figure E6. Click **OK**.

Note: Halftone Pattern

The **Halftone** *Pattern simulates the effect of a halftone screen. This filter maintains the continuous range of tones. This filter can produce three patterns:* **Circle**, **Dot**, *and* **Line** *[see images below].*

Select **Layer 0** and **Layer 1** an then press **Ctrl+E** to merge them. Duplicate **Layer 2** and rename it **Layer 3**. Make sure **Layer 3** is selected and then press **Ctrl+T** to transform. Rotate the layer as shown in Figure E7. Also, scale the image so that it covers whole canvas. Now, press **Enter** to apply the transform. Ensure **Layer 3** is selected in the **Layers** panel and then choose **Blur | Gaussian Blur** from the **Filter** menu. In the **Gaussian Blur** dialog that appears, set **Radius** to **1.6** and then click **OK** [see Figure E8].

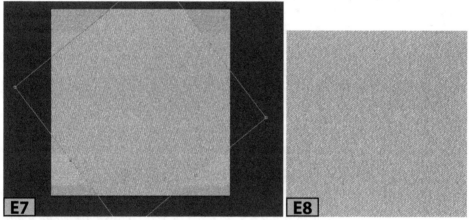

Note: Gaussian Blur Filter

*The **Gaussian Blur** filter blurs [add low frequency details] an image by an adjustable amount. The term **Gaussian** refers to the bell-shaped curve that Photoshop generates when it applies a weighted average to the pixels.*

Set the **Blending Mode** for **Layer 3** to **Linear Light** and **Opacity** to **24%**. Set the **Blending Mode** for **Layer 2** to **Soft Light** [see Figure E9]. Choose **Flatten Image** from the **Layer** menu. Create new layer and rename it as **Layer 4**, fill it with **50%** Gray. Press **D**. Choose **Render | Difference Cloud** from the **Filter** menu. Choose **Adjustment | Equalize** from the **Image** menu [see Figure E10].Choose **Adjustment | Threshold** from the **Image** menu. In the **Threshold** dialog that appears, set **Threshold Level** to **131** and then click **OK** [see Figure E11].

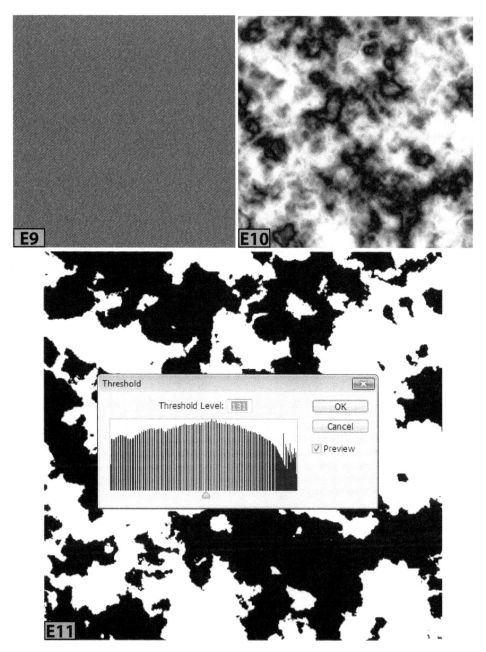

E9

E10

E11

Threshold

Threshold Level: 131

OK

Cancel

☑ Preview

Note: Threshold Filter

*The **Threshold** command converts the images to high-contrast, black-and-white images. All pixels lighter than the threshold value are converted to white; all pixels darker are converted to black.*

Set **Blending Mode** to **Overlay** for **Layer 4** and then set **Opacity** to
18%. Choose **Filter Gallery | Brush Strokes | Simi-e** from the
Filter menu and then use the settings shown in Figure E12. Click
OK. Figure E1 shows the final result.

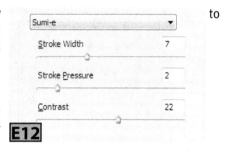

Note: Sumi-e Filter

Sumi-e *is a Japanese style filter. It produces effects like a fully
saturated brush applied to a rice paper. This filter creates soft
blurred edges with rich black.*

Exercise 7: Creating Abstract Texture - I
In this example, you will create an abstract texture, see Figure E1.

The following table summarizes the exercise:

Table E7: Creating Abstract Texture - I	
Skill level	Basic
Time to complete	20 Minutes
Project Folder	**unit-mt1**
Final exercise file	**umt1-hoe-7.psd**
Video	**UMT1VID-HOE-7.MP4**

Create a new **1000x1000 px** Photoshop document and then set the **Foreground Color** to **#00aeef**. Unlock
the **Background** layer and fill it with the **Foreground** color. Apply the **Satin** layer style and set the values
shown in Figure E2. Figure E3 shows the result.

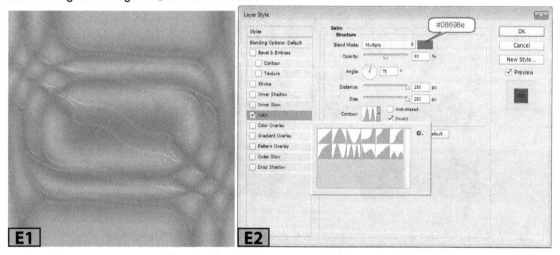

Press **Ctrl+J** to duplicate the layer. RMB click on the layer's name in the **Layers** panel and then choose
Rasterize Layer Style from the popup menu. Choose **Stylize | Trace Contour** from the **Filter** menu. In the
Trace Contour dialog that opens, set **Level** to **128**, **Edge** to **Upper**, and then click **OK** [see Figure E4].

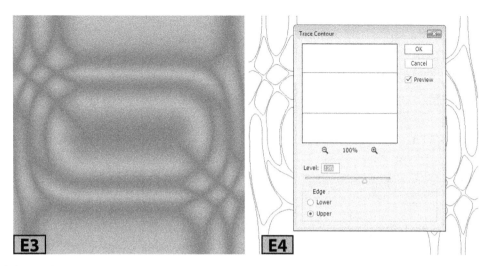

E3 E4

Note: Trace Contour Filter

*The **Trace Contour** filter creates a contour map like effect. It finds transitions between the major brightness areas and then outlines those areas for each color channel.*

Choose **Blur | Motion Blur** from the **Filter** menu. In the **Motion Blur** dialog that opens, set **Angle** to **-40**, **Distance** to **23**, and then click **OK** [see Figure E5]. Set **Blending Mode** to **Divide**. Choose **Distort | Twirl** from the **Filter** menu. In the **Twirl** dialog that appears, set **Angle** to **50** as shown in Figure E6 and then click **OK**. Save the document with the name **umt1-hoe-7.psd**.

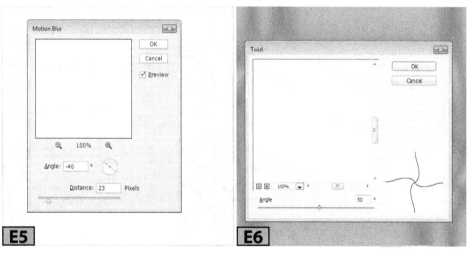

E5 E6

Note: Twirl Filter

This filter rotates a selection. If you specify an angle, it produces a twirl pattern.

Exercise 8: Creating Digital Circuit Board Texture

In this example, you will create a digital circuit board texture, see Figure E1.

The following table summarizes the exercise:

Table E8: Creating Digital Circuit Board Texture	
Skill level	Intermediate
Time to complete	20 Minutes
Project Folder	**unit-mt1**
Final exercise file	**umt1-hoe-8.psd**
Video	**UMT1VID-HOE-8.MP4**

Create a new **1000x1000 px** Photoshop document with the white background. Choose **Convert for Smart Filters** from the **Filter** menu. Choose **Noise | Add Noise** from the **Filter** menu to open the **Add Noise** dialog. In this dialog, set **Amount** to **20**, **Distribution** to **Gaussian**, and the click **OK**.

Ensure the **Monochromatic** switch is on. Choose **Filter Gallery | Sketch | Halftone Pattern** from the **Filter** menu and then set **Size** to **2** and **Contrast** to **4**. Ensure **Dot** is selected as **Pattern Type** and then click **OK** [see Figure E2].

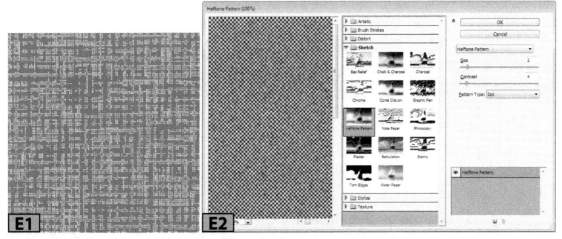

Choose **Filter Gallery | Sketch | Water Paper** from the **Filter** menu and then set **Fiber Length** to **45**, **Brightness** to **76**, and **Contrast** to **71**. Click **OK** [see Figure E3]. Choose **Stylize | Trace Contour** from the **Filter** menu. In the **Trace Contour** dialog that opens, set **Level** to **155**, **Edge** to **Upper**, and then click **OK** [see Figure E4].

Press **Ctrl+A** to select all pixels and then choose **Copy Merged** from the **Edit** menu. Now, press **Ctrl+V**. Create a new layer and place it below **Layer 1**. Fill the layer with the **#58712b** color. Ensure **Layer 0** is selected in the **Layers** panel and then press **Ctrl+I** to invert the layer.

Set **Blending mode** to **Lighten**. Save the document with the name **umt1-hoe-8.psd**.

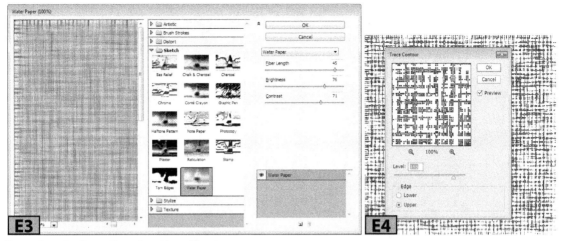

Exercise 9: Creating Leather Texture

In this example, you will create a leather texture, see Figure E1.

The following table summarizes the exercise:

Table E9: Creating Leather Texture	
Skill level	Intermediate
Time to complete	20 Minutes
Project Folder	**unit-mt1**
Final exercise file	**umt1-hoe-9.psd**
Video	**UMT1VID-HOE-9.MP4**

Create a new **1000x1000 px** Photoshop document with the default background and foreground colors. Choose **Filter Gallery | Texture | Stained Glass** from the **Filter** menu and then set **Cell Size** to **5**, **Border Thickness** to **4**, and **Light Intensity** to **2** [see Figure E2]. Click **OK**.

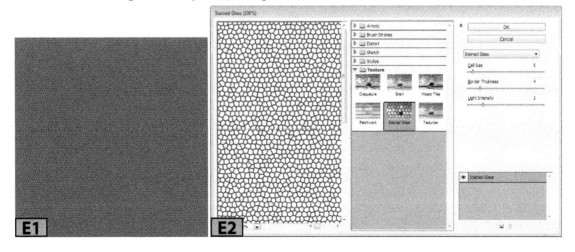

Save the document with the name **umt1-hoe-9.psd**. Save as the document with the name **displaceMap. psd**. Create a new **1000x1000** px Photoshop document and fill it with the **#9D7a51** color. Choose **Filter Gallery | Texture | Texturizer** from the **Filter** menu and then set **Texture** to **Sandstone**, **Scaling** to **60**, and **Relief** to **2**. Select **Light** to **Top** [see Figure E3] and then click **OK**.

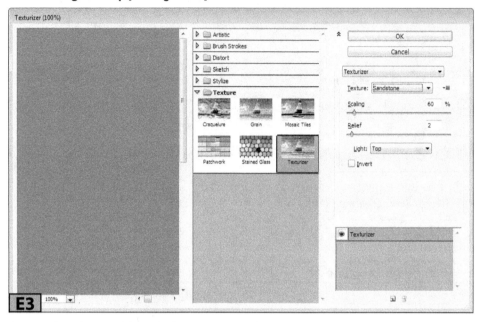

Choose **Filter Gallery | Texture | Texturizer** from the **Filter** menu and then select **Load Texture** from the **Texture** options [see Figure E4]. In the **Load Texture** dialog that appears, select **displaceMap.psd** and then click **Open**. Set **Scaling** to **100**, **Relief** to **4**, and **Light** to **Top Left** [see Figure E5]. Click **OK**. Press **Ctrl+L** and then adjust the levels [see Figure E6]. Save the document.

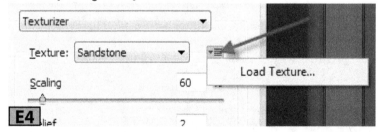

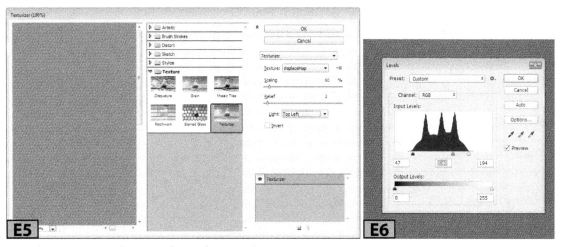

Exercise 10: Creating Lattice Wire Mesh Texture

In this example, you will create lattice wire mesh texture, see Figure E1. The following table summarizes the exercise:

Table E10: Creating Lattice Wire Mesh Texture	
Skill level	Intermediate
Time to complete	20 Minutes
Project Folder	**unit-mt1**
Final exercise file	**umt1-hoe-10.psd**
Video	**UMT1VID-HOE-10.MP4**

Create a new **1000x1000** px Photoshop document with the default background and foreground colors. Unlock the **Background** layer. Choose **Filter Gallery | Texture | Stained Glass** from the **Filter** menu and then set **Cell Size** to **10**, **Border Thickness** to **4**, and **Light Intensity** to **3** [see Figure E2]. Click **OK**.

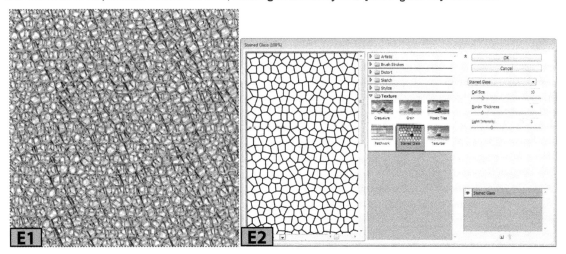

Note: Stained Glass Filter
This filter repaints the image as single colored adjacent cells. The cells are outlined in the foreground color.

Pick **Magic Wand Tool** from **Tool Box** and then click on the black area of the layer. Press **Ctrl+Shift+I** to invert the selection and press **Delete** to remove the pixels [see Figure E3]. Apply the **Bevel and Emboss** layer style to the **Layer 0** and then set the values as shown in Figure E4.

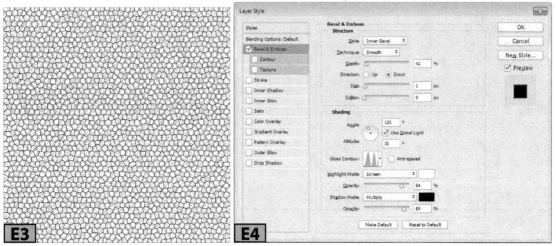

Now, apply **Inner Glow** style, refer Figure E5. Add the **Drop Shadow** style with **Size** and **Distance** set to **2**. Duplicate **Layer 0** and then flip the duplicate layer by choosing **Transform | Flip Horizontal** from the **Edit** menu. Create another copy of the layer and change its position slightly using arrow keys [see Figure E6].

Remove the unwanted portion of the image using the **Crop Tool** and then save the document with the name **umt1-hoe-10.psd**.

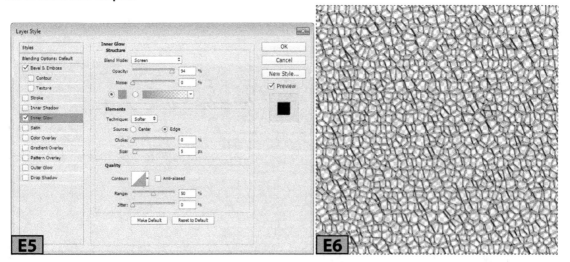

Exercise 11: Creating Brushed Metal Texture

In this example, you will create brushed metal texture, see Figure E1.

E1

The following table summarizes the exercise:

Table E11: Creating Brushed Metal Texture	
Skill level	Intermediate
Time to complete	15 Minutes
Project Folder	**unit-mt1**
Final exercise file	**umt1-hoe-11.psd**
Video	**UMT1VID-HOE-11.MP4**

Create a new **1000x1000 px** Photoshop document with the **50%** gray background. Choose **Noise | Add Noise** from the **Filter** menu to open the **Add Noise** dialog. In this dialog, set **Amount** to **10**, **Distribution** to **Gaussian,** and the click **OK** [see Figure E2]. Choose **Blur | Motion Blur** from the **Filter** menu. In the **Motion Blur** dialog that opens, set **Angle** to **0**, **Distance** to **2000**, and then click **OK** [see Figure E3].

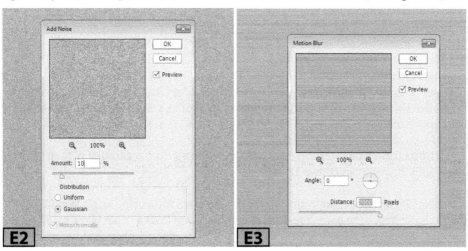

E2　　E3

Save the document with the name **metalDisplace.psd**. Create a new **1000x1000** px Photoshop document with the **50%** gray background. Choose **Noise | Add Noise** from the **Filter** menu to open the **Add Noise** dialog. In this dialog, set **Amount** to **2**, **Distribution** to **Gaussian**, and the click **OK**.

Choose **Filter Gallery | Texture | Texturizer** from the **Filter** menu and then select **Load Texture** from the **Texture** options. In the **Load Texture** dialog that appears, select **metalDisplace.psd** and then click **Open**. Set **Scaling** to **100**, **Relief** to **13**, and **Light** to **Top Left** [see Figure E4]. Click **OK**. Unlock the **Background** layer and apply **Gradient Overlay** style on it, refer Figure E5 for values. Save the document with the name **umt1-hoe-11.psd**.

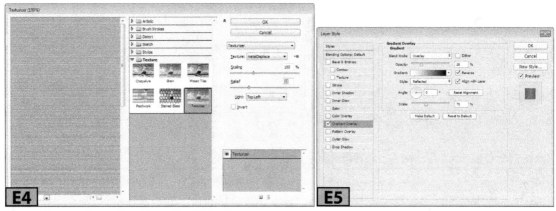

Example 12: Creating Reptile Skin Texture

In this example, you will create reptile skin texture, refer Figure E1. The following table summarizes the exercise:

Table E12: Creating Reptile Skin Texture	
Skill level	Intermediate
Time to complete	30 Minutes
Project Folder	**unit-mt1**
Final exercise file	**umt1-hoe-12.psd**
Video	**UMT1VID-HOE-12.MP4**

Create a new **1000x1000** px Photoshop document and then set the **Foreground** and **Background** colors to default values. Choose **Filter Gallery | Texture | Stained Glass** from the **Filter** menu and then set **Cell Size** to **10**, **Border Thickness** to **4**, and **Light Intensity** to **3**. Click **OK**. Save the document with the name **repltileSkinTexture.psd**.

Create a new **1000x1000** px Photoshop document and then fill the background with the **#86441a**. Save the document with the name **umt1-hoe-12.psd**.

Ensure **repltileSkinTexture.psd** is open and then select the black color using **Magic Wand Tool**. Press **Ctrl+C** to copy the pixels. Switch to the **umt1-hoe-12.psd** and then press **Ctrl+V** to paste the pixels [see Figure E2].

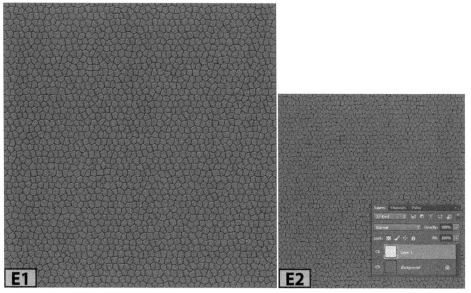

Ensure the **Background** layer is selected and then choose **Filter Gallery | Texture | Texturizer** from the **Filter** menu and then use the **repltileSkinTexture.psd** as **Texture**.

Also, set **Scaling** to **100**, and **Relief** to **3**. Select **Light** to **Top Left** [see Figure E3] and then click **OK**. Select **Layer 1** and apply the **Color Overlay** style to it. Use the **#542103** color.

Figure E4 shows the result. Apply **Bevel & Emboss**, and **Drop Shadow** layer styles [refer Figures E5 and E6 for settings]. Figure E7 shows the result. Press **Ctrl+A** followed by **Ctrl+Shift+C** to copy the merged pixels and then press **Ctrl+V** to paste them. Choose **Filter Gallery | Texture | Texturizer** from the **Filter** menu and then set **Texture** to **Sandstone**, **Scaling** to **100**, and **Relief** to **2**. Select **Light** to **Top** [see Figure E8] and then click **OK**.

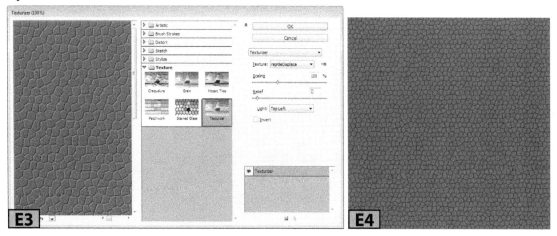

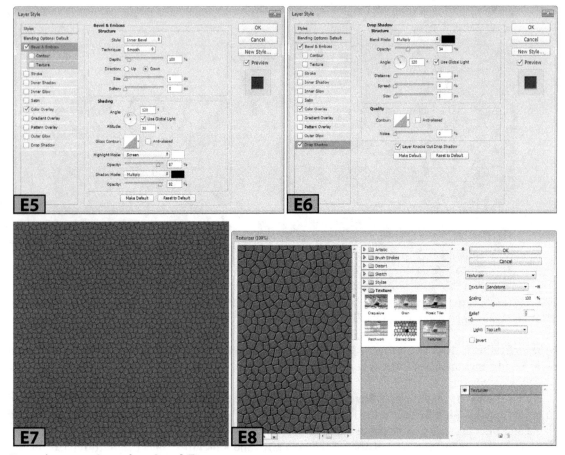

Exercise 13 : Creating Sand Texture

In this example, you will create the sand texture, see Figure E1.

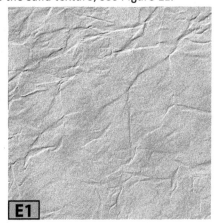

The following table summarizes the exercise:

Table E13: Creating Sand Texture	
Skill level	Intermediate
Time to complete	30 Minutes
Project Folder	**unit-mt1**
Final exercise file	**umt1-hoe-13.psd**
Video	**UMT1VID-HOE-13.MP4**

Create a new **1000x1000** px Photoshop document with and then set the **Foreground** and **Background** colors to default values. Choose **Render | Clouds** from the **Filter** menu.

Note: Clouds Filter
*The **Clouds** filter allows you to create a cloud pattern using the values that transition between the foreground and background colors.*

Tip: Dark cloud pattern
*If you want to create a dark cloud pattern, hold **Alt** and then choose **Render | Clouds** from the **Filter** menu.*

Warning: Clouds Filter
*When you apply the **Clouds** filter, the pixels on the active layer are replaced by the cloud pattern.*

Choose **Noise | Add Noise** from the **Filter** menu to open the **Add Noise** dialog. In this dialog, set **Amount** to **5**, **Distribution** to **Gaussian**, and the click **OK**. Save the document with the name **sandDisplace.psd**. Create a new **1000x1000** px Photoshop document and then set the **Foreground** and **Background** colors as follows: **#c99754** and **#e6c09b**. Choose **Render | Clouds** from the **Filter** menu.

Choose **Filter Gallery | Texture | Texturizer** from the **Filter** menu and then use the **sandDisplace.psd** as **Texture**. Also, set **Scaling** to **100**, and **Relief** to **29**. Select **Light** to **Top Left** [see Figure E2] and then click **OK**. Figure E3 shows the result. Save the document with the name **umt1-hoe-12.psd**.

Open the **crumpledPaper.jpg** and choose **Other | High Pass** from the **Filter** menu. Now, set **Radius** to **165** in the **High Pass** dialog that appears and then click **OK** [see Figure E4]. Save the document as **crumpled-Paper.psd**.

Note: crumpledPaper.jpg
Image Courtesy: *http://capturedbykc.deviantart.com/*
Download Link: *http://www.deviantart.com/art/50-Paper-Textures-Bundle-358150111.*

Switch to **umt1-hoe-13.psd**. Choose **Filter Gallery | Texture | Texturizer** from the **Filter** menu and then use the **crumpledPaper.psd** as **Texture**. Also, set **Scaling** to **144**, and **Relief** to **46**. Select **Light** to **Top Left** [see Figure E5] and then click **OK**. Save the document.

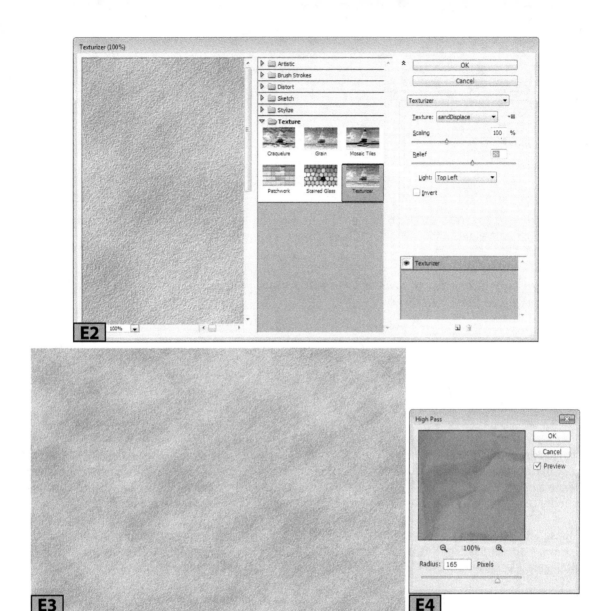

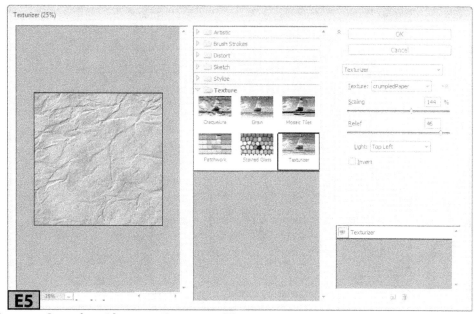

E5

Exercise 14: Creating Abstract Texture - II

In this example, you will create a line art texture, see Figure E1.

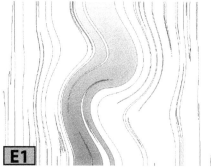

E1

The following table summarizes the exercise:

Table E14: Creating Abstract Texture - II	
Skill level	Intermediate
Time to complete	30 Minutes
Project Folder	**unit-mt1**
Final exercise file	**umt1-hoe-14.psd**
Video	**UMT1VID-HOE-14.MP4**

Open **crumpledPaper.psd**. Choose **Stylize | Emboss** from the **Filter** menu. In the **Emboss** dialog that appears, set **Angle** to **-13**, **Height** to **100**, and **Amount** to **500** [see Figure E2]. Click **OK**.

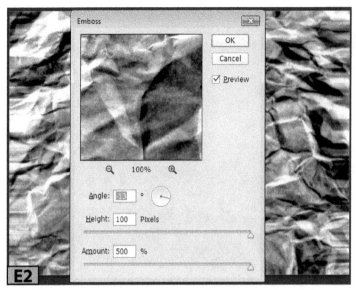

Note: Emboss Filter
This filter makes an image raised or stamped. It converts fill color of the image to gray and traces the edges with the original fill color.

Tip: Fade Command
*If you want to retain the color detailing, use the **Fade** command after applying the **Emboss** filter.*

Choose **Blur | Motion Blur** from the **Filter** menu. In the **Motion Blur** dialog that opens, set **Angle** to **90**, **Distance** to **2000**, and then click **OK** [see Figure E3]. Choose **Distort | Twirl** from the **Filter** menu. In the **Twirl** dialog that appears, set **Angle** to **93** [see Figure E4] and then click **OK**.

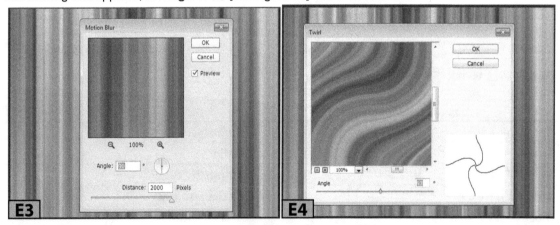

Choose **Stylize | Trace Contour** from the **Filter** menu. In the **Trace Contour** dialog that opens, set **Level** to **132**, **Edge** to **Upper**, and then click **OK** [see Figure E5]. Using the **Magic Wand Tool**, make a selection, refer Figure E6. Create a new layer and fill it with the black color [see Figure E7]. Apply **Gradient Overlay** and **Inner Shadow** layer styles [see Figures E8 and E9] for settings. Save the document with the name **umt1-hoe-14.psd**.

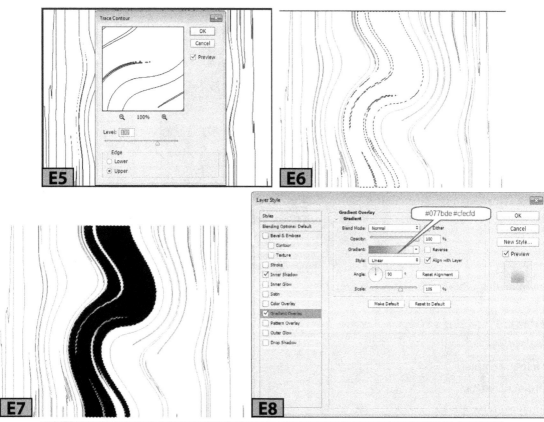

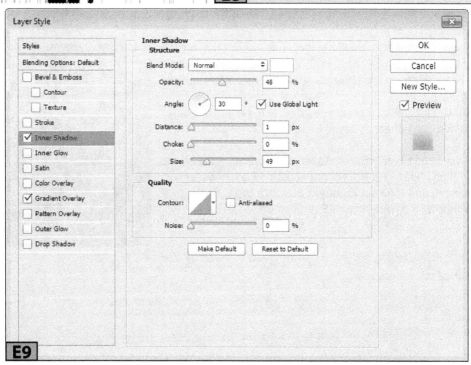

Exercise 15: Creating an Organic Texture

In this example, you will create an organic looking texture, see Figure E1.

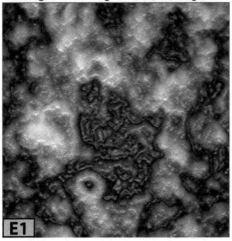

The following table summarizes the exercise:

Table E15: Creating an Organic Texture	
Skill level	Intermediate
Time to complete	30 Minutes
Project Folder	**unit-mt1**
Final exercise file	**umt1-hoe-15.psd**
Video	**UMT1VID-HOE-15.MP4**

Create a new **1000x1000** px Photoshop document then set the **Foreground** and **Background** colors to default values. Choose **Render | Difference Clouds** from the **Filter** menu. Apply this filter multiple time by pressing **Alt+Ctrl+F**, until you get a nice pattern [refer Figure E2]. Unlock the **Background** layer. Create two more copies of **Layer 0** and name them as **Layer 1** and **Layer 2**, respectively.

Turn on **Layer 1** and **Layer 2**. Ensure **Layer 0** is selected in the **Layers** panel and then choose **Filter Gallery | Artistic | Plastic Wrap** from the **Filter** menu and then set **Highlight Strength** to **11**, **Detail** to **9**, and **Smoothness** to **6** [refer Figure E3]. Click **OK**.

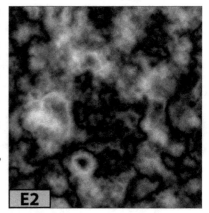

Note: Plastic Wrap Filter
This filter wraps the image in the shiny plastic, making the surface detail more noticeable.

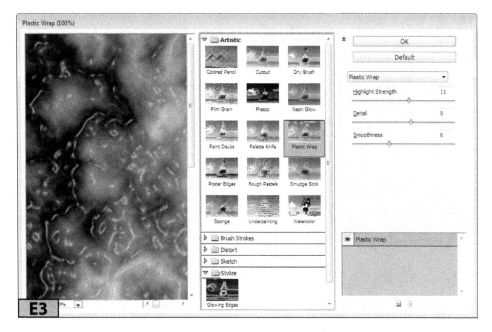

Turn on **Layer 1** and select it in the **Layers** panel. Choose **Stylize | Emboss** from the **Filter** menu. In the **Emboss** dialog that appears, set **Angle** to **90**, **Height** to **4**, and **Amount** to **500** [see Figure E4]. Click **OK**.

Set **Blending Mode** to **Overlay** for **Layer 1**. Now, select **Layer 2** and make it visible. Choose **Filter Gallery | Artistic | Paint Daubs** from the **Filter** menu and then set **Brush Size** to **10**, **Sharpness** to **3**, and **Brush Type** to **Simple** [refer Figure E5].

Click **OK**. Set **Blending Mode** to **Lighten** for **Layer 2**. Figure E6 shows the result.

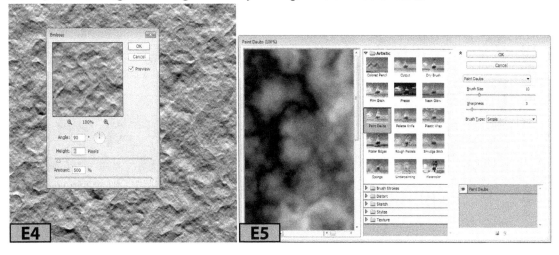

Note: Paint Daubs Filter

This filter produces a painterly effect using different brushes. The available brushes are **Simple**, **Light Rough**, **Dark Rough**, **Wide Sharp**, **Wide Blurry**, *and* **Sparkle** *[refer to images given below].*

Select **Layer 0** and then choose **Blur | Gaussian Blur** from the **Filter** menu. In the **Gaussian Blur** dialog that opens, set **Radius** to **3** and then click **OK** [see Figure E7]. Save the document with the name **umt1-hoe-15.psd**.

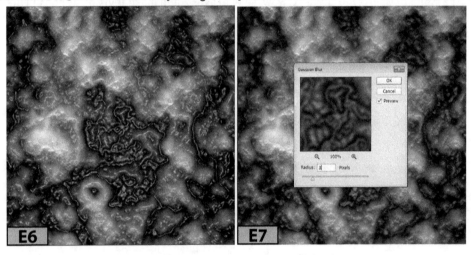

Exercise 16: Creating Backgrounds - 1

In this example, you will create a background, as shown in Figure E1.

The following table summarizes the exercise:

Table E16: Creating Backgrounds - 1	
Skill level	Intermediate
Time to complete	25 Minutes
Project Folder	**unit-mt1**
Final exercise file	**umt1-hoe-16.psd**
Video	**UMT1VID-HOE-16.MP4**

Open **carinaNebula.jpg**. Choose **Calculations** from the **Image** menu. In the **Calculations** dialog that opens, set **Channel** to **Blue** in the **Source 1** section. Set **Channel** to **Red** from the **Source 2** section. Set **Blending** to **Overlay**. Also, ensure that **New Channel** is selected from the **Result** drop-down [see Figure E2]. Click **OK**.

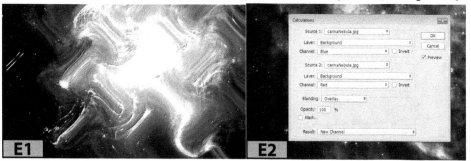

Note: Calculations Command
*The **Calculations** command allows you to blend two individual channels from one or more source images. You can apply results to a new image, new selection, or selection in the active image.*

Warning: Calculation Command
If you are using two source images, the images must have the same pixel dimensions.

Switch to the **Channels** panel. Ensure that the **Alpha 1** channel is selected [see Figure E3]. Press **Ctrl+A** and then **Ctrl+C** to copy the channel data. Now, select **RGB** channel layer. Now, select **RGB** channel. Switch back to the **Layers** panel and then press **Ctrl+V** to paste the data [see Figure E4].

Set the **Foreground** and **Background** colors to **#8f2c00** and **#b93904**, respectively. Create a new layer and place it under the pasted layer and then using **Gradient Tool** fill the layer. Set **Blending Mode** to **Linear Light** for the **Layer 1** [see Figure E5]. Ensure **Layer 1** is selected and then choose **Lens Flare** from the **Filter | Render** menu. In the **Lens Flare** dialog that opens, place the hotspot as shown in Figure E6, and then click **OK**. Figure E7 shows the result. Choose **Distort | Wave** from the **Filter** menu. In the **Wave** dialog that appears, set the values, shown in Figure E8 and then click **OK**.

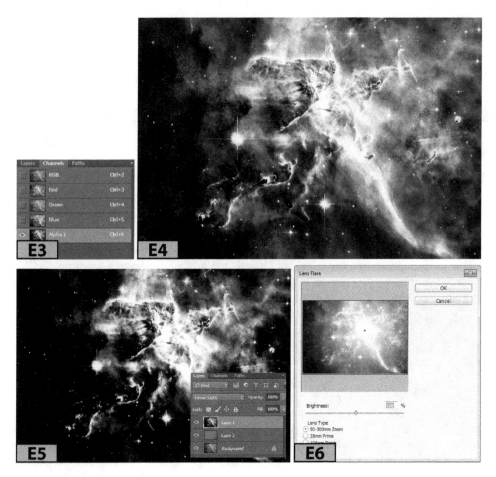

Note: Lens Flare

The **Lens Flare** filter allows you to simulate the refraction caused by shining a bright light into a camera lens.

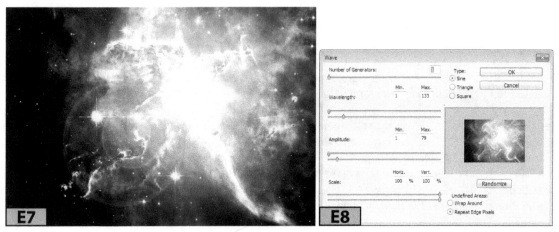

Note: Wave Filter

*This filter is like the **Ripple** filter but it provides better control. It creates an undulating pattern on a selection.*

Press **Ctrl+J** to duplicate **Layer 1** and then choose **Stylize | Emboss** from the **Filter** menu. In the **Emboss** dialog that appears, set **Angle** to **135**, **Height** to **3**, and **Amount** to **100** [see Figure E9]. Click **OK**. Save the document with the name **umt1-hoe-16.psd**.

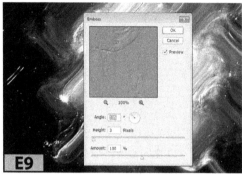

Exercise 17: Creating Backgrounds - 2

In this example, you will create a background, as shown in Figure E1.

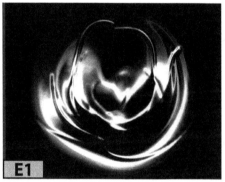

The following table summarizes the exercise:

Table E17: Creating Backgrounds - 2	
Skill level	Intermediate
Time to complete	30 Minutes
Project Folder	**unit-mt1**
Final exercise file	**umt1-hoe-17.psd**
Video	**UMT1VID-HOE-17.MP4**

Create a new **1000x1000** px Photoshop document and fill it with black. Create a new layer and fill it with black as well. Choose **Lens Flare** from the **Filter | Render** menu. Set the values in the **Lens Flare** dialog that opens, as shown in Figure E2 and then click **OK**.

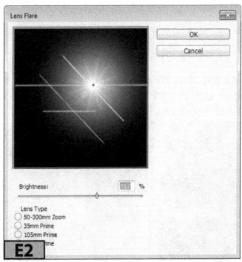

E2

Press **Ctrl+J** to create a duplicate layer and then choose **Transform | Flip Horizontal** from the **Edit** menu. Set **Blending Mode** to **Screen** [see Figure E3]. Merge the upper two layers. Choose **Distort | Wave** from the **Filter** menu. In the **Wave** dialog that appears, set the values, shown in Figure E4 and then click **OK**.

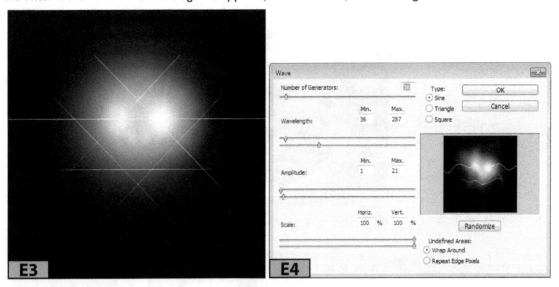

E3

E4

Choose **Distort | Polar Coordinates** from the **Filter** menu. In the **Polar Coordinates** dialog that appears, select **Rectangular to Polar** and then click **OK** [see Figure E5].

Note: Polar Coordinates Filter
This filter can be used to create a cylinder anamorphosis, a form of art popular in the 18th century. It converts a selection from rectangular to polar coordinates and visa-versa.

Choose **Filter Gallery | Sketch | Chrome** from the **Filter** menu and then set **Detail** to **5** and **Smoothness** to **7**. Click **OK** [see Figure E6].

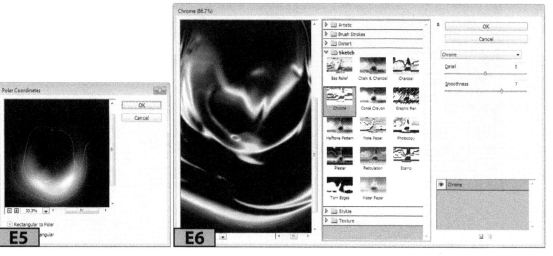

Note: Chrome Filter

This filter allows you to render the image as if it had a polished chrome surface. The areas with highlights are raised whereas areas with shadows appear lower.

Tip: Chrome Filter

*If you are using this filter, use the **Levels** adjustment to add more contrast to the image.*

Add a **Curves** adjustment layer and adjust the curve [see Figure E7].

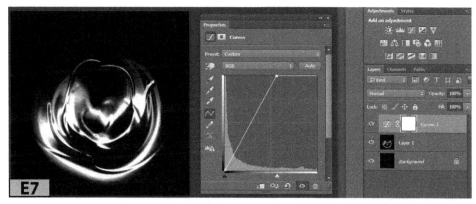

Now, add a **Hue and Saturation** adjustment layer and check the **Colorize** check box in the **Properties** panel. Adjust the **Hue** slider to give the design some color [see Figure E8]. Save the document with the name **umt1-hoe-17.psd**.

Exercise 18: Creating Backgrounds - 3

In this example, you will create a background, as shown in Figure E1.

The following table summarizes the exercise:

Table E18: Creating Backgrounds - 3	
Skill level	Intermediate
Time to complete	20 Minutes
Project Folder	**unit-mt1**
Final exercise file	**umt1-hoe-18.psd**
Video	**UMT1VID-HOE-18.MP4**

Create a new **1000x1000** px Photoshop document. Press **D** to set the **Foreground** and **Background** colors to default. Choose **Render | Clouds** from the **Filter** menu. Unlock the **Background** layer.

Choose **Filter Gallery | Sketch | Chrome** from the **Filter** menu and then set **Detail** to **0** and **Smoothness** to **10** [see Figure E2]. Click **New Effect Layer** and click **Sketch | Plaster** [see Figure E3] and then click **OK**.

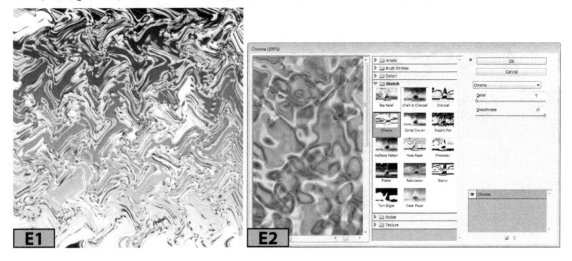

Choose **Distort | Wave** from the **Filter** menu. In the **Wave** dialog that appears, set the values, as shown in Figure E4 and then click **OK**.

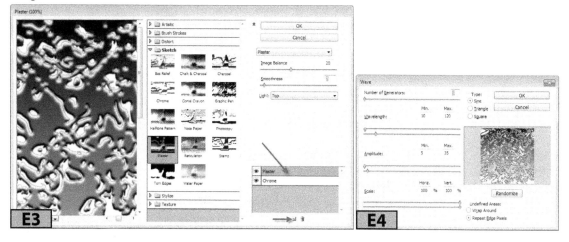

Figure E5 shows the result. Press **Ctrl+J** to create the duplicate of **Layer 0**. Choose **Distort | Wave** from the **Filter** menu. In the **Wave** dialog that appears, click **Randomize** then click **OK**. Set the blending mode to **Lighten**. Add a **Color Balance** adjustment layer and then set the values as shown in Figure E6. Save the document with the name **umt1-hoe-18.psd**.

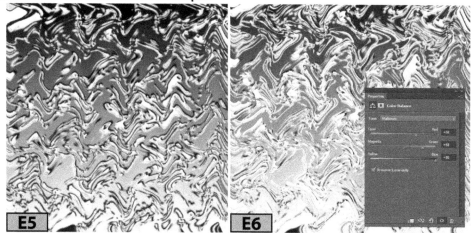

Exercise 19: Creating Backgrounds - 4

In this example, you will create a background, as shown in Figure E1. The following table summarizes the exercise:

Table E19: Creating Backgrounds - 4	
Skill level	Intermediate
Time to complete	30 Minutes
Project Folder	**unit-mt1**
Final exercise file	**umt1-hoe-19.psd**
Video	**UMT1VID-HOE-19.MP4**

Google the following term: **stephen quentent hubble**, then download the image. Open the downloaded image in Photoshop. Unlock the **Background** layer. Choose **Filter Gallery | Sketch | Chrome** from the **Filter** menu and then set **Detail** to **0** and **Smoothness** to **10** [see Figure E2].

Create two copies of **Layer 0** and rename them as **Layer 1** and **Layer 2**. Turn off **Layer 2** and then select **Layer 1**. Choose **Distort | Wave** from the **Filter** menu. In the **Wave** dialog that appears, accept the default values and then click **OK**. Change blending mode to **Lighten** [see Figure E3].

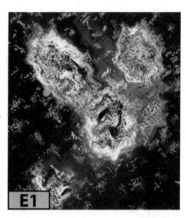

Select **Layer 2** and turn it on. Choose **Distort | Wave** from the **Filter** menu. In the **Wave** dialog that appears, click **Randomize** couple of times to get a different pattern and then click **OK**. Set blending mode to **Screen**. Merge the layers and then apply the **Extrude** filter to get some interesting results.

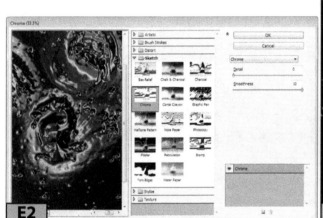

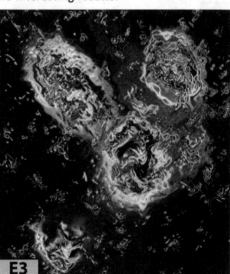

Exercise 20: Creating Backgrounds - 5

In this example, you will create a background, as shown in Figure E1.

The following table summarizes the exercise:

Table E20: Creating Backgrounds - 5	
Skill level	Intermediate
Time to complete	30 Minutes
Project Folder	**unit-mt1**
Final exercise file	**umt1-hoe-20.psd**
Video	**UMT1VID-HOE-20.MP4**

Start a new **1280x720** px document and then fill the background layer with black. Create a new layer. Set the **Foreground** color to white and then choose a large splatter brush and click once to paint the stroke [see Figure E2]. Apply the **Color Overlay** style to the **Layer 1** [see Figure E3]. Use the following color: **4eff00**.

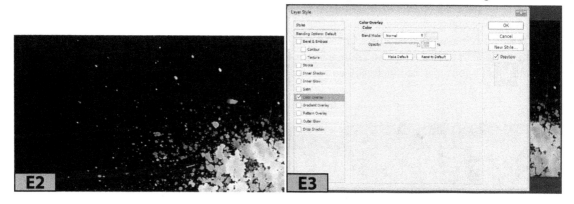

Press **Ctrl+J** to duplicate **Layer 1** and rename it is **Layer 2**. Select **Layer 2** and choose **Blur | Motion Blur** from the **Filter** menu. In the **Motion Blur** dialog that appears, set **Angle** to **90** and **Distance** to **2000**. Click OK [see Figure E4]. Choose **Distort | Twirl** from the **Filter** menu. In the **Twirl** dialog that appears, set **Angle** to **150** and click **OK** [see Figure E5]. Select **Layer 2** and press **Ctrl+J** to create a duplicate and rename is as **Layer 3**. Select **Layer 2** and **Layer 3** and press **Ctrl+E** to merge them.

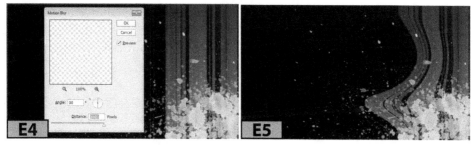

Select **Layer 1** and then choose **Distort | Twirl** from the **Filter** menu. In the **Twirl** dialog that appears, set **Angle** to **150** and click **OK**. Choose **Distort | Wave** from the **Filter** menu. In the **Wave** dialog that appears, set the values as shown in Figure E6 and then click **OK** [See Figure E7]. Duplicate **Layer 3** and rename duplicate as **Layer 4**. Select **Layer 3** and choose **Blur | Gaussian Blur** from the **Filter** menu. In the **Gaussian Blur** dialog that opens, set **Radius** to **20** and click **OK**.

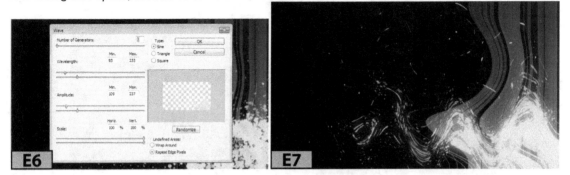

Select **Layer 3** and **Layer 4**. Press **Ctrl+E** to merge the layers. Apply the **Wave** filter to the **Layer 4** use the same settings as before [see Figure E8]. Set **Opacity** of **Layer 1** to **20%**. Merge **Layer 1** and **Layer 4**. RMB click on **Layer 4** and choose **Blending Options**. In the **Layer Style** dialog that appears, click **Styles**. Load **KS Styles** and then click on the forth style [see Figure E9]. Click **OK**.

Press **Ctrl+A** to select all pixels. Press **Ctrl+Shift+C** to copy the merged pixels and then press **Ctrl+V** to paste them. Select **Layer 5** and then choose **Blur | Gaussian Blur** from the **Filter** menu. In the **Gaussian Blur** dialog that opens, set **Radius** to **0.5** and click **OK**. Save the file with the name **umt1-hoe-20.psd**.

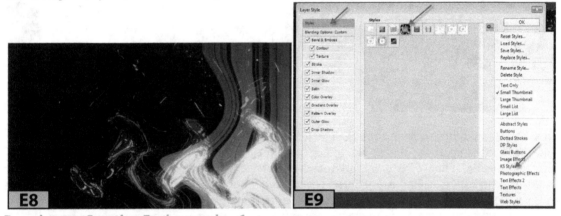

Exercise 21: Creating Backgrounds - 6

In this example, you will create a background, as shown in Figure E1.

The following table summarizes the exercise:

Table E21: Creating Backgrounds - 6	
Skill level	Intermediate
Time to complete	20 Minutes
Project Folder	**unit-mt1**

Final exercise file	umt1-hoe-21.psd
Video	UMT1VID-HOE-21.MP4

Create a new **1000x1000** px document. Choose **Render | Fibers** from the **Filter** menu. In the **Fibers** dialog that appears, set the values as shown in Figure E2 and click **OK**.

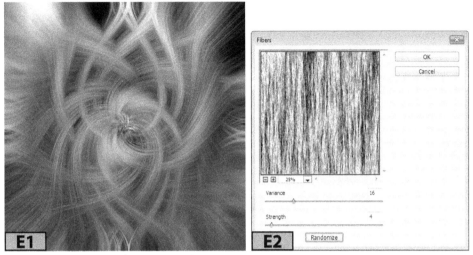

Choose **Filter Gallery | Sketch | Plaster** from the **Filter** menu. Set the values as shown in Figure E3 and then click **OK**. Choose **Filter Gallery | Brush Strokes | Sprayed Strokes** from the **Filter** menu.

Set the values as shown in Figure E4 and then click **OK**. Choose **Blur | Radial Blur** from the **Filter** menu. In the **Radial Blur** dialog that opens, set the values as shown in Figure E5, and then click **OK**. Figure E6 shows the result.

Make two copies of the **Background** layer and rename them as **Layer 1** and **Layer 2**. Select **Layer 1** and then choose **Distort | Twirl** from the **Filter** menu. In the **Twirl** dialog that appears, set **Angle** to **158** and then clock **OK**. Select **Layer 2** and then choose **Distort | Twirl** from the **Filter** menu. In the **Twirl** dialog that appears, set **Angle** to **-158** and then clock **OK**.

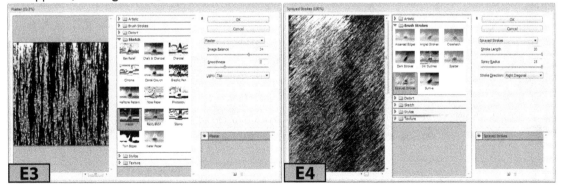

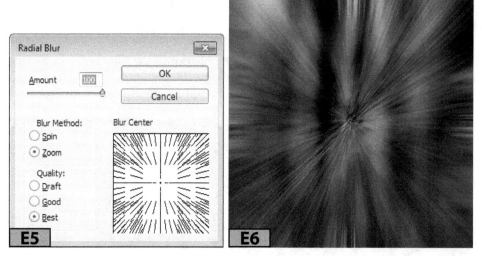

Select **Layer 2** and set its **Blending Mode** to **Lighten**. Press **Ctrl+U**. In the **Hue/Saturation** dialog that appears, set the values as shown in Figure E7 and then click **OK**. Select **Layer 1** and set its **Blending Mode** to **Lighten**. Press **Ctrl+U**. In the **Hue/Saturation** dialog that appears, set the values as shown in Figure E8 and then click **OK**.

Select **Layer 1** and press **Alt+Shift+Ctrl+L**. Repeat the process for **Layer 2**. Save the document with the name **umt1-hoe-21.psd**.

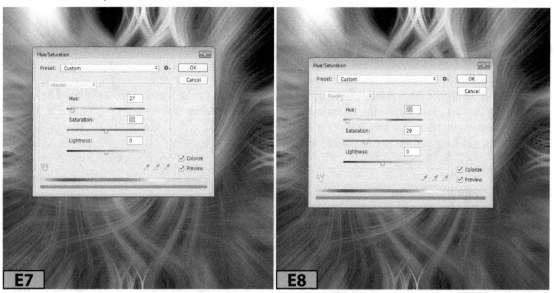

Quiz

Evaluate your skills to see how many questions you can answer correctly.

Multiple Choice

Answer the following questions, only one choice is correct.

1. Which of the following hotkeys is used to change the color of the foreground and background swatches to their default colors?

    [A] **F**   [B] **B**
    [C] **D**   [D] **H**

2. Which of the following hotkeys is used to merge the layers?

    [A] **Ctrl+M**   [B] **Ctrl+C**
    [C] **Ctrl+E**   [D] **Ctrl+H**

3. Which of the following hotkeys is used to invoke **Levels** command?

    [A] **Ctrl+L**   [B] **Ctrl+F**
    [C] **Ctrl+H**   [D] **Ctrl+R**

Fill in the Blanks

Fill in the blanks in each of the following statements:

1. The _____ layers non-destructively alter underlying tones and colors.

2. _____ in Photoshop are used to hide portions of a layer or reveal the portions of the layers below

3. The _____ filter randomly generates values between the foreground and background colors to create a cloud pattern.

4. The _____ filter allows you to retain the edge details in the specified radius where sharp color transitions occur in the image.

5. The _____ command redistributes the brightness values so that they represent entire range of the brightness values.

6. The _____ command/adjustment layer allows you to make adjustment to the tonal range and color balance of an image.

True or False

State whether each of the following is true or false:

1. To clip an adjustment layer to affect only one layer in the **Layers** panel, hold **Alt** and then move the mouse pointer on the boundary of the two layers.

2. If you select a layer and then choose **Convert for Smart Filters** from the **Filter** menu, the selected layer is converted to a smart object and then you can apply smart filters onto the smart object.

3. Photoshop does not flatten the images, if you switch between the color modes.

4. The **Threshold** command converts the images to high-contrast, black-and-white images.

Summary

In this unit, the following topics are covered:

- Understanding non-destructive editing
- Creating custom textures and designs
- Creating maps

Unit MT2 - Material Editors

A material editor is a window that allows you to create, and edit materials as well as to assign them to the objects in the scene. A material in 3ds Max defines how light is reflected and transmitted by the objects in a scene.

In the unit, I will describe the following:

- **Compact Material Editor**
- **Slate Material Editor**

3ds Max offers two material editors, **Compact Material Editor** and **Slate Material Editor**. These editors offer a variety of the functions and features that allow you to design realistic looking surfaces in 3ds Max. To open an editor, choose **Compact** 🪟 or **Slate** ✕ option from the **Material Editor** flyout on the **Main** toolbar. You can also open an editor by choosing **Compact Material Editor** or **Slate Material Editor** from the **Rendering** menu | **Material Editor** sub-menu | **Compact Material Editor/Slate Material Editor**.

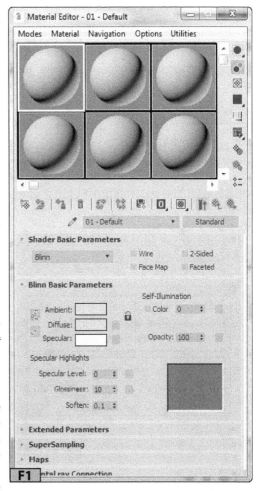

Compact Material Editor

This was the only material editor available prior to the 2011 release of 3ds Max. It is comparatively a small window [see Figure F1] than the **Slate Material Editor** window and allows you to quickly preview the material. If you are assigning materials that have already been designed, this material editor is the preferred choice.

Note: Additional Features

*Compact Material Editor has some options such as **Video Color Check** and **Custom Sample Objects** that are not available in **Slate Material Editor**.*

The **Compact Material Editor's** interface consists of menu bar at the top [see Figure F1], sample slots below the menu bar, and toolbars at the bottom and right of the sample slots. Now onwards, I will refer to these toolbars as horizontal and vertical toolbars, respectively. The interface also consists of many rollouts. The content on these rollouts depends on the active material slot and the type of material it hosts.

Note: Switching Editors
*If you want to switch to **Slate Material Editor**, choose **Slate Material Editor** from the editor's **Modes** menu.*

Sample Slots

The sample slots allow you to preview material and maps. By default, six sample slots appear in the editor. You can increase the number of slots by choosing **Cycle 3x2, 5x3, 6x4 Sample Slots** from the editor's **Options** menu. This option cycles through the 3x2, 5x3, and 6x4 slots arrangement. To make a sample slot active, click on the sample slot. The active sample slot appears with a white border around it.

Caution: Maximum number of sample slots
***Compact Material Editor** allows you to edit up to 24 materials at a time. However, the scene can contain an unlimited numbers of materials. When you finish a material and apply it to the objects in the scene, you can use the slot occupied by that material to design the next material.*

By default, material appears on a sphere geometry in a sample slot. You can change the sphere to cylinder or cube by choosing the desired option from the **Sample Type** flyout. This flyout is the first entry in the editor's vertical toolbar. To view a magnified version of the sample slot in a floating window, double-click on it. You can resize the window to change the magnification level of the sample slot.

Hot and Cool Materials

A sample slot is considered to be hot if it is assigned to one or more surfaces in the scene. When you use the editor to adjust properties of a hot material, the changes are reflected in the viewport at the same time. The corners of a sample slot indicates whether the material is hot or not. Here're the possibilities:

No triangle: The material is not used in the scene.
Outlined white triangle: The material is hot and the changes you make to it will change the material displayed in the scene.
Solid white triangle: The material is not only hot but it is also applied to the currently selected object in the scene.

Notice the three sample slots in Figure F2 that show three possibilities: a hot material applied to the currently selected, a hot material is applied to the scene but not on the currently selected object, and a cool material which is active but not assigned to scene, respectively. If you want to make a hot material cool, click **Make Material Copy** from the horizontal toolbar. You can have the same material with the same name in multiple slots but only one slot can be hot. However, you can have more than one hot sample slots as long as each sample slot has a different material.

F2

If you drag a material to copy it from one sample slot to another, the destination slot will be cool whereas the original slot remains hot.

When you RMB click on a sample slot, a popup menu appears. Table 1 summarizes the options available in this menu.

Table 1: Sample slot RMB click menu	
Option	**Description**
Drag/Copy	This is active by default. When active, dragging a sample slot copies the material from one sample slot to another.
Drag/Rotate	When you select this option, dragging the sample slot rotates the sample geometry in the slot. This is useful in visualizing the map in the slot.
Reset Rotation	Resets the sample slot's rotation.
Render Map	Opens the **Render Map** dialog that allows you to render the current map. You can create an **AVI** file if the map is animated.
Options	Opens the material editor's options.
Magnify	Generates a magnified view of the current sample slot.
Select By Material	Selects objects based on the material in the sample slot.
Highlight Assets in the ATS dialog	This option is typically used for the bitmap textures. It opens the **Asset Tracking** dialog with the assets highlighted.
Sample Windows Options	You can use these options to change the number of slots displayed in the material editor.

Managing Materials with the Compact Material Editor

By default, the **Standard** material is displayed when you select a sample slot. If you want to use the **Standard** material, you can choose the desired shading model from the drop-down available in the **Shader Basic Parameters** rollout of the editor and then assign colors or maps to the various components of the material. For example, if you want to assign a map to the **Diffuse** component of the material, click on the button located at the right of the **Diffuse** color swatch to open the **Material/Map Browser** which is a modeless dialog. From the browser, select the map from the **Maps | General/Scanline/Environment** rollout and then click **OK**.

Tip: Material Map Browser
You can also double-click on a map to select it and close the browser.

For example, if you want to apply a checker map, double-click on the **Checker** map from the **Maps | General** rollout of the browser. Once you select the map, 3ds Max shows rollouts in the editor that you can use to edit the properties of the map. To go back to the parent level, click **Go To Parent** from the horizontal toolbar.

You can also copy map from one component to another component. For example, you have applied a map to the **Diffuse** component of the material and you want to copy it to **Opacity** component. Drag the **Diffuse's** button onto the **Opacity's** button, the **Copy (Instance) Map** dialog appears. Select the desired option from the **Method** group and then click **OK** to create an instance, a copy, or just to swap the materials from one slot to another.

Note: Other materials
*If you want to use any other material than the **Standard** material, click on **Type** button [labelled as **Standard**] to open the **Material/Map Browser**. Double-click on the desired material from the **Materials | General/Scanline** rollout; the **Replace Material** dialog appears with options to discard the old material or keep the old material as a sub-material. Choose the desired option and click **OK**. The label **Standard** on the button will be replaced by the type of the new material. For example, if you have chosen **Blend**, the **Standard** label will be replaced by the **Blend** label.*

By default, 3ds Max gives a name to each material. This appears name below the horizontal toolbar. If you want to change the name, edit the name in the field. The name field only displays 16 characters but the material name can be longer than 16 characters.

If the material you want to change is present in the scene but is not displayed in any of the sample slots, you can get it directly from the scene. To do this, select the object in the scene and click a sample slot to make it active. From the horizontal toolbar, click **Get Material** ⊛ to open **Material/Map Browser**. Find the scene material in the **Scene Materials** rollout and then double-click on the name of the material. You can also drag the material name to the sample slot. When you get a material from the scene, it is initially a hot material.

To apply a material to the objects in the scene, drag the sample slot that contains the material to the object[s] in the scene. If there is only one object selected in the scene, the material is immediately applied to that object. If there are more than one objects in the scene, 3ds Max prompts you to choose whether to apply the material to the single object or to the whole selection. You can also apply material to the selection by clicking **Assign Material To Selection** ⊛ on the horizontal toolbar. Once you apply material to objects in the scene, click **Show Shaded Material in Viewport** ⊛ on the horizontal toolbar to view the material on the objects in the scene.

Tip: Hot material
When you apply a material to an object, the material becomes a hot material.

Tip: Removing material from an object
*To remove a material from an object, select the object and then execute the following command from the **MAXScript Listener**: $.material=undefined.*

Note: Selecting objects that have the same material applied
*From the vertical toolbar, click **Select By Material** ⊛. This button will not be available unless the active sample slot contains a material that is applied to the objects in the scene. The **Select Objects** dialog appears. Those objects onto which the material has been applied appear highlighted in the dialog. Click **Select** to select the objects in the scene.*

You can also save a material to the library. A material library helps you in organizing materials. You can use a material from a library in another scene, if required. To save a material to the library, on the horizontal toolbar, click **Put To Library** , the **Put To Library** dialog appears. In this dialog, change the name of the material or leave as is. Click **OK** to save the material. The material is saved in the currently opened library. If no library is open, a new library is created. You can save this library as a file using **Material/Map Browser** controls.

To get a material from the library, click **Get Material** to open **Material/Map Browser**. Now, open a library group. In the list of the materials in the library, double-click on the name of the material that you intend to use. The material you choose from the library replaces the material in the active sample slot.

Material/Map Browser

The **Material/Map Browser** [see Figure F3] allows you to choose a material or map. When you click the **Type** button or any button on the **Compact Material Editor**, a modal version of **Material/Map Browser** opens.

Note: Slate Material Editor
*In **Slate Material Editor**, **Material/Map Browser** appears as a panel and always visible.*

At the top-left corner of the browser, the **Material/Map Browser Options** button ▼ is available. When you click this button, a menu is displayed from where you can set various options for **Material/Map Browser**. The **Search by Name** field on the right of the button allows you to filter the maps and materials in the browser. For example, if you type **grad** in the field and press **Enter**, the maps and materials will be displayed below the field whose names start with the characters **grad** [see Figure F4].

The main part of the browser is the list of materials and maps arranged in the rollouts [groups]. You can collapse or expand these groups.

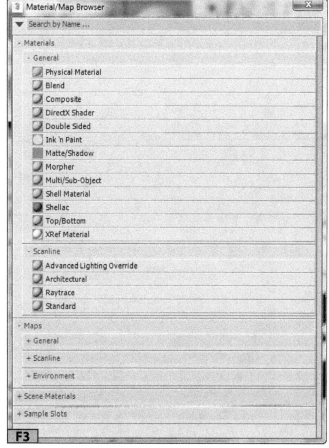

Caution: Materials and maps in the Material/Map Browser

*By default, **Material/Map Browser** only displays those maps and materials that are compatible with the active renderer.*

Note: Material/Map Browser's contextual menu

When you RMB click on the header of a rollout, a popup menu appears [see Figure F5]. This menu shows the general options related to that particular group.

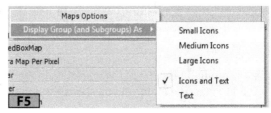

Material Explorer

The **Material Explorer** [see Figure F6] allows you to browse and manage all materials in a scene. You can open the explorer from the **Rendering** menu. You can also open it as an extended viewport. To do this, choose **Material Explorer** from the **Point-Of-View (POV) Viewport** label menu | **Extended Viewports**.

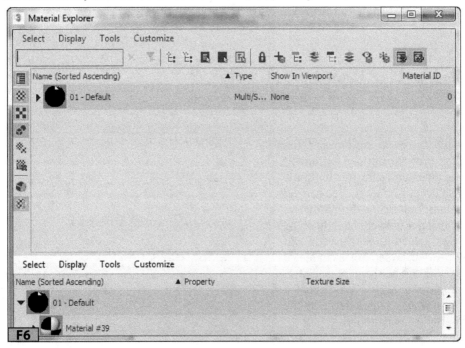

Compact Material Editor lets you set the properties of the materials but there is limitations on number of materials it can display at a time. However, with **Material Explorer**, you can browse all the materials in the scene. You can also see the objects onto which the materials are applied, you can change the material assignment, and manage materials in other ways.

Slate Material Editor

Slate Material Editor is little complex than **Compact Material Editor**. In this editor, the entities are displayed in form of nodes that you can wire together to create material trees. If you are working on a large scene with lots of materials, this editor is the preferred choice. The powerful search function provided by this editor lets you find materials in a complex scene easily.

I mostly use **Slate Material Editor** as its interface [see Figure F7] is more intuitive when it comes to designing materials. I have marked various components of the interface with numbers in Figure F7. Table 2 summarizes **Slate Material Editor's** interface.

Number	Description
Table 2: The **Slate Material Editor's** interface overview	
Number	Description
1	Menu bar
2	Toolbar
3	Material/Map Browser
4	Status
5	Active View
6	View navigation
7	Parameter Editor
8	Navigator

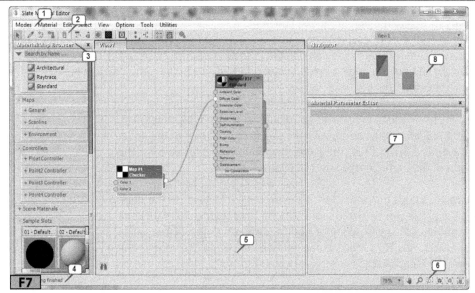

There are three main visual elements of **Slate Material Editor: Material/Map Browser, Active View,** and **Parameter Editor. Active View** is the area where you create material trees and make connections between nodes using wires. **Parameter Editor** is the area where you adjust settings of maps and materials. You can float the components of the editor such as **Material/Map Browser,** or **Parameter Editor** [except view]. For example, to float the **Material/Map Browser,** double-click on its title. To dock it back to the editor, again double-click on its title.

Note: Preview window

By default, each material preview window opens as a floating window. When you dock a material preview window, it docks to the upper left area of the editor.

When you add materials or maps in **Slate Material Editor**, they appear as nodes [see left image in Figure F8] in the active view.

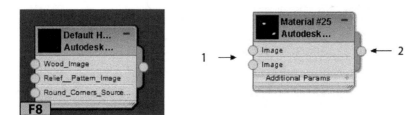

You can then connect these nodes using wires to make material trees. A node has several components, here's is a quick rundown.

- The title bar of the node shows name of the material or map, material or map type, and a small preview icon of the material or map.
- Below the title bar the component of the material or map appears. By default, 3ds Max shows only those components that you can map.
- On the left side of each component a circular slot [marked as 1 in the right image of Figure F8] is available for input. You can use these sockets to wire maps to the node.
- On the right of the node, a circular slot [marked as 2 in the right image of Figure F8] that is used for the output.

You can collapse a node to hide its slots. To do this, click on the minus sign [marked as 1 in Figure F9] available on the upper right corner of the node. To resize a node horizontally, drag the diagonal lines available on the bottom-right of the node [marked as 2 in Figure F9].

When you resize a node horizontally, it's easier to read the name of the slots. To change the preview icon size,double-click on the preview. To reduce the preview, double-click again. When a node's parameters are displayed in **Parameter Editor**, 3ds Max shows a dashed border around the node in the active view [see Figure F10].

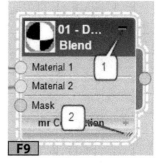

To create a new material, drag the material from **Material/Map Browser** to the active view, 3ds Max places a node for the material in the active view. It is a good habit to change the name of the material immediately. It will make your life easier if you are working on a complex scene with tons of materials. To rename a material, RMB click on it and choose **Rename**. In the **Rename** dialog, change the name of the material and click **OK**. To change the properties of the material, double-click the node in the active view and then change the properties from **Parameter Editor**.

The name of a material can contain special characters, numbers, and spaces.

To get a material from the scene, click **Pick Material From Object** 🖋 from the toolbar. Now, click on the object in a viewport to get the material. To apply a material to objects in the scene, drag the output socket of the node and then drop the wire on an object in the scene. As you drag the mouse in a viewport, a tooltip appears below the mouse pointer showing the name of the object. You can apply the material even if the object is not selected. If there is only one object selected in the scene, the material is immediately applied to that object. If there are more than one objects in the scene, 3ds Max prompts you to choose whether to apply the material to the single object or to the whole selection. You can also apply material to the selection by clicking **Assign Material To Selection** on the toolbar.

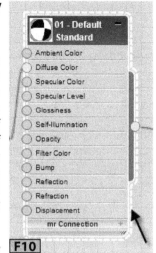

To make a copy of the existing material, drag the material from the **Material/ Map Browser | Scene Materials** group (or any library) to the active View. The **Instance (Copy)** dialog appears. Select **Instance** or **Copy** from this dialog and click **OK**. To duplicate a node in the active view, select the node[s] that you want to duplicate and then drag the nodes with the **Shift** held down.

To select the objects onto which you have applied the same material, in the active view, select the node and then click **Select By Material** 🔍 from the toolbar. 3ds Max opens the **Select Objects** dialog with the objects highlighted. Click **Select** to select the highlighted objects.

Selecting, Moving, and Laying Out Nodes

To select a node, ensure **Select Tool** ▶ [hotkey **S**] is active, and then click on the node. To select multiple nodes, click on the nodes with the **Ctrl** held down. If you want to remove nodes from the selection, click on the nodes with **Alt** held down. To select all nodes, press **Ctrl+A**. To invert the selection, press **Ctrl+I**. To select none of the nodes, press **Ctrl+D**. To select children, press **Ctrl+C**. To select a node tree, press **Ctrl+T**. These functions are also accessible from the **Select** menu of the editor.

Note: Selected node

When a node is selected in the view, a white border appears around it. Also, the background including the title bar is darker. When node is not selected, the border appears gray and background is lighter.

Tip: Deselecting nodes

*To deselect nodes, click on the blank area of the view using **Select Tool** ▶.*

To move a node, drag it in the active view. To create clone of a node, drag it with the **Shift** held down. If you drag a node with **Ctrl+Shift** held down, 3ds Max clones the node and all its children. These methods also work on multiple selections.

If you want to move a node and its children, click **Move Children** from the toolbar and drag a node. You can toggle this feature temporarily without clicking **Move Children** by moving the node with **Ctrl+Alt** held down. This feature can be accessed from the editor's **Options** menu. You can click the **Hide Unused Nodeslots** ⬚ option from the toolbar to hide the unused ports on the selected material.

The layout buttons on the toolbar allow you to arrange nodes in the active view. The **Layout All - Vertical** ⬚ and **Layout All - Horizontal** ⬚ buttons on the toolbar allow you to arrange nodes in an automatic layout along the vertical or horizontal axis in the active view. These options are also available in the editor's **View** menu. The **Layout Children** button allows you to automatically layout the children of the selected node.

If you turn on the **Show Shaded Material In Viewport** ⬚ from the toolbar for a material, a red diagonal shape appears on the node in the active view [see the left image in Figure F11]. **Navigator** also shows a red diagonal shape to indicate this [see the middle image in Figure F11]. This shape also appears in the **Scene Materials** rollout of the **Material/Map Browser** [see the right image in Figure F11].

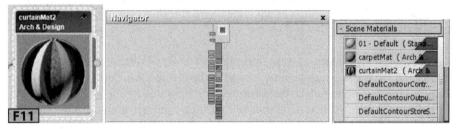

Previewing Materials

The **Preview** window [see Figure F12] of the editor allows you to visualize how material or map will appear in the scene. The main part of the window is a rendering of the material or map. You can resize this window like you resize any other window in 3ds max that is, by dragging its corners. Making a window larger helps you in visualizing the material, however, larger previews take longer to render. To open this window, RMB click on a node and then choose **Open Preview Window** from the popup menu.

To close a window, click **X** on the upper-right corner of the window. By default,a sphere is displayed as a sample geometry in the scene. If you want to change this geometry, choose **Cylinder** or **Box** from **RMB click** menu | **Preview Object Type** sub-menu. You can open any number of **Preview** windows in the editor. However, the drop-down available at the bottom of the **Preview** window allows you to switch the previews in a single window.

Caution: Preview window
*When open a new scene, the **Preview** window remains open, however, it may not correspond to any material. I recommend that you close all **Preview** windows before creating a new scene. The previews are not saved with the scene.*

When the **Auto** switch is on in the **Preview** window, 3ds Max automatically renders the preview again when you make any changes to the properties of a material or map. When this switch is off, the **Update** button becomes active. The render will be displayed only when you click **Update**. The **Show End Result** toggle available on the right of **Update** allows you to control when the **Preview** window displays a map.

When off , the **Preview** window shows the map itself. When on, the **Preview** window shows the end result that is, the final result of the node.

Wiring Nodes

As you already know, wires are used to connect material or map components. To understand the wiring process, from the **Material/Map Browser | Materials** rollout | **General** rollout, drag **Standard** to the active view to create a **Standard** material node. Similarly, drag **Checker** from the **Material/Map Browser | Maps** rollout | **General** rollout to the active view to create a **Checker** node [see left image in Figure F13]. Click-drag the **Standard** material's **Diffuse Color** socket, a wire appears. Now, drop the wire on the output socket of the **Checker** node to make a connection [see the right image in Figure F13]. You can also connect in reverse. You can connect the output socket of the **Checker** node to the **Diffuse Color** slot of the **Standard** material.

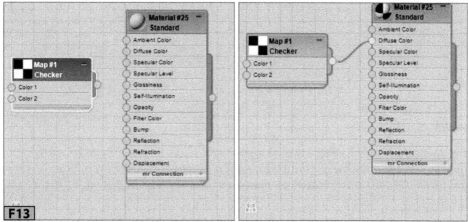

F13

Now, drag and the **Standard** material's **Bump** socket to the blank area, a popup menu appears [see the left image in Figure F14], choose **Standard | Noise** from the menu to insert a **Noise** node and make connection between the **Noise** node and **Bump** socket of the **Standard** material [see the right image in Figure F14].

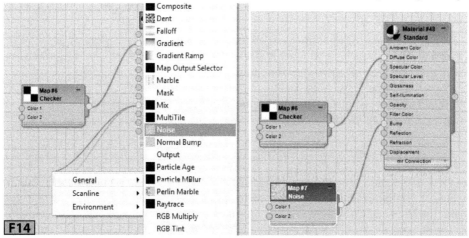

F14

You can also connect a map directly to a socket without first dragging to the active view. To do this, drag the **Falloff** map from the **Material/Map Browser | Maps** rollout | **General** rollout to the **Reflection** socket of the **Standard** material. When the socket turns green, release the mouse to make the connection [see

Figure F15]. Another way to connect a node to a socket is to double-click on a socket to open **Material/Map Browser**. Now, select the desired map or material from the browser. You can also drag a wire on the title bar of a node. A popup menu appears [see Figure F16] that allows you to select component to wire.

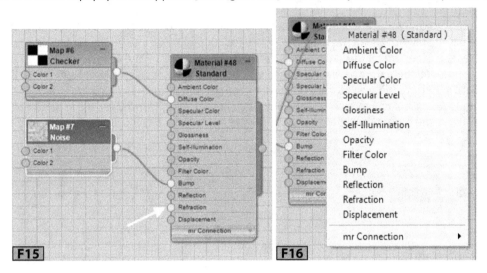

To delete a connection [wire], select the wire and then press **Delete**. The selected wire appears in white color. You can also drag away a wire from a socket where it has been connected to terminate the connection. To replace one map with another, drag from the new map's output socket to the output socket of the original map.

To insert a node into a connection, drag the node from the **Material/Map Browser** and then drop it on the wire. You can also drag from one of the node's input sockets to the wire to insert the node. If a node is lying on the active view and you want to insert it, drop the node on the wire with **Ctrl** held down. To disconnect an inserted node, drag the node and then press **Alt** while dragging.

When you RMB click on a wire, a popup menu appears [see Figure F17]. Choose **Change Material/Map Type** to open **Material/Map Browser** and then choose a different type for the material or map. This option always affects the child node. The **Make Node Unique** option makes the child unique if the child node is instanced. The **Make Branch Unique** makes the child unique, as well as duplicates children of the child if the child node is instanced.

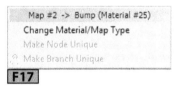

Views

The active view is the main area of **Slate Material Editor** where all action takes place. The navigating the active view is similar to the navigating a scene in 3ds Max. To pan the view, drag with the MMB. If you drag with the MMB and **Ctrl+Alt** held down, 3ds max zooms the view. You can also zoom by scrolling the wheel. The navigational tools are also available at the bottom-right corner of the editor's interface.

Table 3 summarized these controls.

Table 3: **Slate Material Editor** navigational controls		
Control	**Hotkey[s]**	**Menu**
Zoom percentage drop-down list	-	
Pan Tool	Ctrl+P	View | Pan Tool
Zoom Tool	Alt+Z	View | Zoom Tool
Zoom Region Tool	Ctrl+W	View | Zoom Region Tool
Zoom Extents	Ctrl+Alt+Z	View | Zoom Extents
Zoom Extents Selected	Z	Zoom Extents Selected
Pan to Selected	Alt+P	View | Pan to Selected

If you are working on a complex scene, you might face difficulties locating nodes in the active view. You can use the search function of the editor to locate the nodes in the scene. Make a habit of renaming the nodes as you create them so that you can find the nodes using their names. To search a node, click the **Search For Nodes** button available on the bottom-left corner of the active view, 3ds Max expands the search tool. Type the name of the node in the search field and press **Enter** to locate the node and zoom on the node in the active view.

By default, **Navigator** appears on the upper-right corner of **Slate Material Editor**. This window is most useful when you have lots of material trees displayed in the active view. This window shows a map of the active view. The red rectangle in the navigator shows the border of the active view. If you drag the rectangle, 3ds max changes the focus of the view.

Named Views
If you are working on a complex scene, you can create named views to organize materials in a scene. You can create any number of views in the editor and then make one of them the active view. When you open the editor in a new scene, a single view is displayed with the name **View1**. To manage views, RMB click on one of the tab and then choose the desired options from the popup menu displayed [see Figure F18].

To cycle through the tabs, use the **Ctrl+Tab** hotkeys. You can also select a view from the drop-down available above **Navigator**. To move a tree from one view to another, RMB click on the node and then choose **Move Tree to View** | **Name of the View** from the popup menu.

Quiz

Evaluate your skills to see how many questions you can answer correctly.

Multiple Choice

Answer the following questions, only one choice is correct.

1. Which of the following keys is used to invoke **Select Tool** in **Slate Material Editor**?

    [A] **K**   [B] **H**
    [C] **S**   [D] **N**

2. Which of the following hotkeys is used to invoke **Zoom Tool**?

    [A] **Ctrl+Z**   [B] **Shift+Z**
    [C] **Alt+Z**   [D] **Ctrl+Shift+Z**

Fill in the Blanks

Fill in the blanks in each of the following statements:

1. When the _____ switch is on in the **Preview** window, 3ds Max automatically renders the preview again when you make any changes to the properties of a material or map.

2. To delete a connection [wire], select the wire and then press _____.

3. To cycle through the tabs in **Active View**, use the _____ hotkeys.

True or False

State whether each of the following is true or false:

1. **Compact Material Editor** allows you to edit up to 36 materials at a time.

2. A sample slot in **Compact Material Editor** is considered to be hot if it is assigned to one or more surfaces in the scene.

3. In **Compact Material Editor**, If you drag a material to copy it from one sample slot to another, the destination slot will be cool whereas the original slot remains hot.

Summary

The unit covered the following topics:

*   **Compact Material Editor**
*   **Slate Material Editor**

Unit MT3 - Standard Materials and Maps

The **Standard Materials** materials are non-photometric materials. Do not use these materials if you plan to create physically accurate lighting models. However, these materials are suitable for games, films, and animation. In this unit, we are going to look at the standard materials and maps.

In this unit, I'll describe the following:

- Standard materials
- Standard maps

General/Scanline Materials

Let's explore the **Scanline** materials.

Standard Material

A surface having a single color reflects many other colors such as ambient, diffuse, and specular. The **Standard** materials use a four-color model to simulate the reflected colors from a surface. However, there may be variations depending on the shader you use. The **Ambient** color appears where surface is lit (the surface in the shadow) by the ambient light only. The **Diffuse** color appears on the surface when the lights falls directly on it. The term **Diffuse** is used because light is reflected in various directions. The **Specular** color appears in the highlights. Highlights are reflection of light sources on the surface.

Generally, shiny surfaces have specular highlights where the viewing angle is equal to the angle of incident. Metallic surfaces show another type of highlights called glancing highlights. The glancing highlights have a high angle of incidence. Some surfaces in the real-world are highly reflective. To model such surfaces, you can use a reflection map or use raytracing. **Filter Color** is the color transmitted through an object. **Filter Color** will only be visible, if **Opacity** is less than **100** percent.

The three color components blend at the edge of their respective regions. The blend of the **Diffuse** and **Ambient** components is controlled by the shader. However, you can control the blending by using the **Standard** material's highlight controls.

To create a **Standard** material, press **M** to open **Slate Material Editor**. On the **Material Editor | Material /Map Browser | Materials | Scanline** rollout, double-click **Standard** to add a standard material node to the active view. Figure F1 shows the **Standard** material's interface. If you double-click on the material node, its attributes appear in various rollouts on **Parameter Editor**. The controls on these rollouts change according to the shader type chosen from the **Shader Basic Parameters** rollout [see Figure F2].

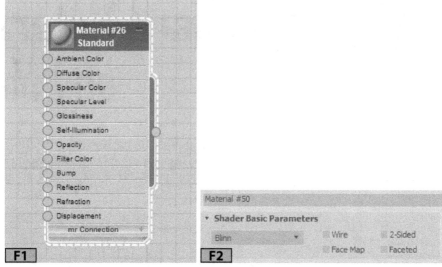

F1

F2

The controls in this rollout let you choose the type of shader to use with the **Standard** material. **Wire** lets you render the material in the wireframe mode [see Figure F3]. You can change the size of the wire using the **Size** control on the material's **Extended Parameters** rollout. Figure F4 shows the render with **Size** set to **2**. **2-Sided** allows you to make a 2-sided material. When you select this option, 3ds Max applies material to the both sides of the selected faces.

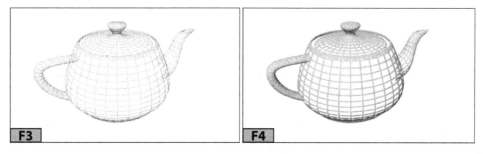

F3

F4

Note: One-sided faces

In 3ds Max, faces are one-sided. The front side is the side with the surface normals. The back side of the faces is invisible to the renderer. If you see this other side from the back, the faces will appear to be missing.

The **Face Map** control allows you to apply the material to the faces of the geometry. If material is a mapped material, it requires no mapping coordinates and automatically applied to each face. Figures F5 and F6 show the render with the **Face Map** switch is in off and on states, respectively. The **Faceted** control renders each face of the surface as if it were flat [see Figure F7].

F5

F6

F7

MT3-2   **Unit MT3 - Standard Materials and Maps**

Tip: Rendering both sides of a face
*There are two ways to render both sides of a face. Either you can turn on **Force 2-Sided** in the **Render Setup** dialog | **Common** panel | **Options** section or apply a two sided material to the faces.*

The **Shader** drop-down located at the extreme left of the rollout lets you choose a shader for the material.

Here's is the quick rundown to the various material shaders:

Phong Shader
You can use this shader to produce realistic highlights for shiny, and regular surfaces. This shader produces strong circular highlights. This shader can accurately render bump, opacity, shininess, specular, and reflection maps. When you select the **Phong** shader, the **Phong Shader Parameters** rollout appears in the material's **Parameter Editor** [see Figure F8].

Phong Shader Parameters Rollout
The controls in this rollout let you set the color of the material, shininess, and transparency of the material. The **Ambient**, **Diffuse**, and **Specular** controls let you set the colors for ambient, diffuse, and specular color components, respectively. To change a color component, click on the color swatch and then use the **Color Selector** to change the values of the color component. You can also copy one color component to another by dragging the source color swatch to the target color swatch. In the **Copy or Swap Colors** dialog that appears, click **Swap**, or **Copy** button. Click **Cancel** to cancel the operation. You can lock or unlock two color components using the **Lock** button [see Figure F9].

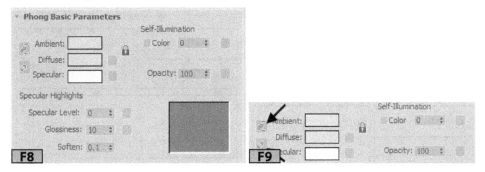

The buttons located on the right of color swatches can be used to apply texture maps to the respective color components. On clicking these buttons, **Material/Map Browser** appears that allows you to select a map for the color component. If you want to apply different maps to the **Ambient** and **Diffuse** components, click on the **Lock** button located to the right of these components [see Figure F10].

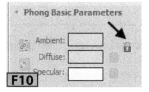

Self-Illumination Group: You can use the controls in this group to make the material self-illuminated. The illusion of self-illumination is created by replacing shadows with the diffuse color. There are two ways to enable self-illumination in 3ds Max. Either you can turn on the switch located in this group and use a self-illumination color or use the spinner.

Note: Self-illuminated materials
Self-illuminated materials do not show shadows cast onto them. Also, they are unaffected by the lights in the scene.

Opacity Group: You can use the controls in this group, to make a material opaque, transparent, or translucent. To change the opacity of the material, change opacity to a value less than 100%. If you want to use a map for controlling opacity, click **Opacity** map button.

Specular Highlight Group: The **Phong**, **Blinn**, and **Oren-Nayar-Blinn** shaders produce circular highlights and share same highlight controls. The **Blinn** and **Oren-Nayar-Blinn** shaders produce soft and round highlights than the **Phong** shader. You can use the **Specular Level** control to increase or decrease the strength of a highlight. As you change the value for this control, the **Highlight** curve and the highlight in the preview changes. The shape of this curve affects the blending between the specular and diffuse color components of the material. If the curve is steeper, there will be less blending and the edge of the specular highlight will be sharper. To increase or decrease the size of the highlight, change the value for **Glossiness**. **Soften** softens the specular highlights especially those formed by the glancing light.

Extended Parameters Rollout

The **Extender Parameters** rollout [see Figure F11] is same for all shaders except **Strauss** and **Translucent** shaders. The controls in this rollout allow you to control the transparency and reflection settings. Also, it has controls for adjusting the wireframe rendering.

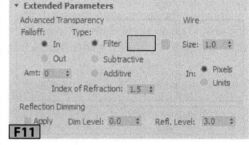

Advanced Transparency Group: These controls do not appear for the **Translucent** shader. **Falloff** allows you to set the falloff and its extent. **In** increases transparency towards the inside of the object (like glass bottle) whereas **Out** increases transparency towards the outside of the object (like clouds). **Amt** lets you adjust the amount of transparency at the outside or inside extreme.

The **Type** controls let you specify how transparency is applied. The **Filter** color swatch computes a filter color that it multiplies with the color behind the transparent surface. The **Subtractive** option subtracts from the color behind the transparent surface. The **Additive** option adds to the color behind the transparent surface.

Index of Refraction allows you to set the index of refraction used by refraction map and raytracing.

Reflection Dimming group: This group does not appear for the **Strauss** shader. These controls dim the reflection in the shadows. Tun on the **Apply** switch to enable reflection dimming. **Dim Level** controls the amount of dimming that takes place in shadow. **Refl. Level** affects the intensity of the reflection that is not in shadow.

SuperSampling Rollout

The **SuperSampling** rollout [see Figure F12] is used by the **Architectural**, **Raytrace**, **Standard**, and **Ink 'n Paint** materials to improve the quality of the rendered image. It performs an additional antialiasing pass on the material thus resulting in more render time. By default, a single **SuperSampling** method is applied to all materials in the scene.

Maps Rollout: The **Maps** rollout [see Figure F13] is available for all materials. The controls in this rollout allow you to assign maps to various components of a material. To assign a map to a component, click the corresponding map button. Now, choose the desired map option from **Material/Map Browser** that opens.

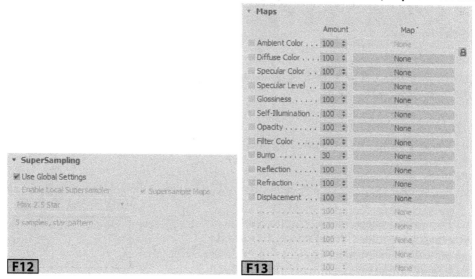

Blinn Shader

This is the default shader. It produces rounder, softer highlights than the **Phong** shader. The **Blinn** and **Phong** shaders have the same basic parameters.

Metal Shader

You can use the **Metal** shader to create realistic-looking metallic surfaces and a variety of organic-looking materials. The metal material calculates their specular color automatically. The output specular color depends on the diffuse color of the material and the color of the light.

This shader produces distinctive highlights. Like the **Phong** shader, **Specular Level** still controls intensity. However, **Glossiness** affects both the intensity and size of the specular highlights. Figure F14 shows the controls in **Metal Basic Parameters** rollout.

Oren-Nayar-Blinn Shader

This shader is a variant of the **Blinn** shader and can be used to model matte surfaces such as fabric. It has two additional controls to model a surface with the matte look: **Diffuse Level** and **Roughness**.

[**Oren-Nayar-Blinn Basic Parameters** rollout | **Advanced Diffuse** group]: **Diffuse Level** controls [see Figure F15] the brightness of the diffuse component of the material. It allows you to make the material lighter or darker. **Roughness** allows you to control the rate at which the diffuse component blends into the ambient component.

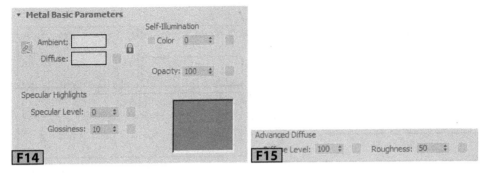

Note: The Roughness Parameter

The **Roughness** parameter is available only with the **Oren-Nayar-Blinn** and **Multi-Level** shaders, and with the **Physical** material.

Note: Diffuse Level control

The **Blinn, Metal, Phong,** and **Strauss** shaders do not have the **Diffuse Level** control.

Strauss Shader

This shader is a simpler version of the **Metal** shader. It can be used to model the metallic surfaces.

Strauss Basic Parameters Rollout: The **Color** control [see Figure F16] lets you specify the color of the material. The **Strauss** shader automatically calculates the ambient and specular color components. **Glossiness** controls the size and intensity of the specular highlights. On increasing the value for this control, the highlight gets smaller and the material appears shiner. The **Metalness** control adjust the

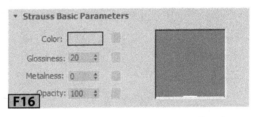

metalness of the surface. The effect of this control is more prominent when you increase the **Glossiness** value. **Opacity** sets the transparency of the material.

Anisotropic Shader

You can use this shader to create surfaces with elliptical, anisotropic highlights. This shader is suitable for modeling hair, glass, or brushed metal. The **Diffuse Level** control is similar to that of the **Oren-Nayar-Blinn** shader, and basic parameters controls are similar to that of the **Blinn** or **Phong** shading, except the **Specular Highlights** parameters.

Anisotropic Basic Parameters rollout | **Specular Highlight** group: The **Specular Level** [Figure F17] control sets the intensity of the specular highlights. On increasing the value for this control, the highlight goes brighter. **Glossiness** controls the size of the specular highlights. **Anisotropy** controls the anisotropy or shape of the highlight. **Orientation** controls the orientation of the highlight. This value is measured in degrees.

Multi-Layer Shader

This shader is similar to the **Anisotropic** shader. However, it allows you to layer two sets of specular highlights. The highlights are layered that allows you to create complex highlights. Figure F18 shows the two specular layers in the **Multi-Layer Basic Parameters** rollout.

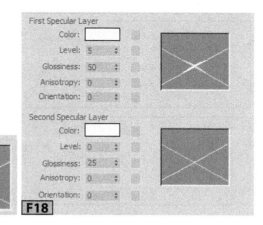

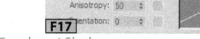

F17

F18

Translucent Shader

This shader is similar to the **Blinn** shader but allows you set the translucency of the material. A translucent object not only allows light to pass through but it also scatters light within.

Translucent Basic Parameters rollout | **Translucency** group: The **Translucent Clr** control [see Figure F19] sets the translucency color that is the color of the light scattered within the material. This color is different from the **Filter** color which

F19

is the color transmitted through transparent or semi-transparent material such as glass. The **Opacity** control sets the opacity or transparency of the material.

Raytrace Material

This material is an advanced surface-shading material. It supports the same diffuse surface shading that a **Standard** material supports.

However, it also supports fog, color density, translucency, fluorescence, and other special effects. This material is capable of creating fully raytraced reflections and refractions. Figure F20 shows the **Raytrace** material's interface.

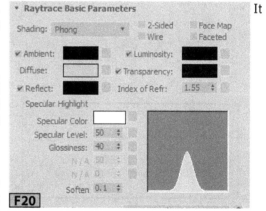

F20

Architectural Material

The properties of this material [see Figure F21] create realistic looking images when used with Photometric lights and **Radiosity**. Therefore, you should use this material when you are looking for high level of accuracy. If you don't need the high detail this material produces, use the **Standard** material or any other material.

When you create a new **Architectural** material, you can choose from a wide variety of templates that are built into this material. You can use these templates as starting point for the shading model you wish to create. You can choose template from the drop-down available in the **Templates** rollout.

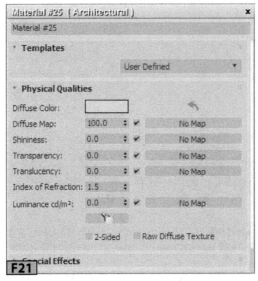

F21

Advanced Lighting Override Material

You can use this material to directly control the radiosity properties of a material. You can use this material directly. It is a always a supplement to the base material [see Figure F22]. This material has no effect on the ordinary renderings. It is used with **Radiosity** and **Light Tracing** solutions.

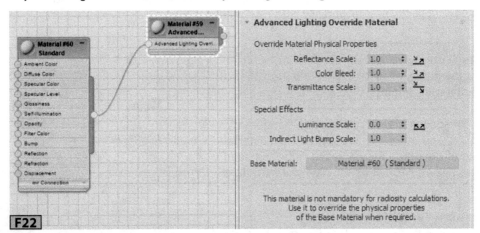

F22

This material has two primary usages:

- Adjusting properties of a material used in a **Radiosity** and **Light Tracing** solutions.
- Contributing energy to the **Radiosity** solution with self-illuminating objects.

General Materials

Let's explore the **General** materials.

Blend Material

The **Blend** material allows you to mix two materials on a single side of the surface. You can use the **Mix Amount** parameter [see Figure F23] to control the way two materials are blended together. You can also animate this control. The **Material 1** and **Material 2** controls let you assign the two materials to be blended. You can also use the corresponding switches to turn material on or off. The **Interactive** option specifies which of the materials or mask map will be displayed in the viewport by the interactive renderer.

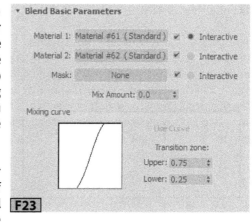

The **Mask** control lets you assign a map as mask. The lighter and darker areas on the mask map control the degree of blending. The lighter areas displays more of the **Material 1** whereas the darker areas show more of **Material 2**. The **Mix Amount** controls the proportion of blend in degrees. A value of **0** means only **Material 1** will be visible on the surface whereas a value of **100** means **Material 2** will be visible on the surface.

When you assign a mask map for blending, you can use the mixing curve to affect the blending. You can use the controls in the **Transition Zone** group to adjust the level of the **Upper** and **Lower** limits.

Note: Interactive renderer and Blend material
Only one map can be displayed in the viewports when using the interactive renderer.

Note: Blend Material and Noise Map
*The **Mix Amount** control is not available when you use mask to blend the material. Using a **Noise** map as mixing map can produce naturally looking surfaces.*

Double Sided Material

The **Double Sided** material lets you assign two different materials to the front and back surface of an object. The **Facing Material** and **Back Material** controls [see Figure F24] allow you to specify the material for the front and back faces, respectively. The **Translucency** control allows you to blend the two materials. There will be no blending of

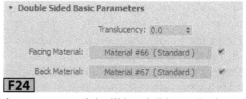

the materials if **Translucency** is set to **0**. At a value of **100**, the outer material will be visible on the inner faces and inner material will be visible on the outer faces.

Composite Material

This material can be used to composite up to ten materials. The materials are composited from top to bottom. The maps can be combined using additive opacity, subtractive opacity, or using an amount value. The **Base Material** control [see Figure F25] allows you to set the base material. The default base material is the **Standard** material.

The **Mat.1** to **Mat.9** controls are used to specify the material that you want to composite. Each material control has an array of buttons called **ASM** buttons. These buttons control how the material is composited. The **A** button allows you to use the additive opacity.

The colors in the materials are summed based on the opacity. The **S** button allows you to use the subtractive opacity. The **M** button is used to mix the materials using a value. You can enter the value in the spinner located next to the **M** button. When the **M** button is active, amount ranges from **0** to **100**. When amount is **0**, no compositing happens and the material below is not visible. If the amount is **100**, the material below is visible.

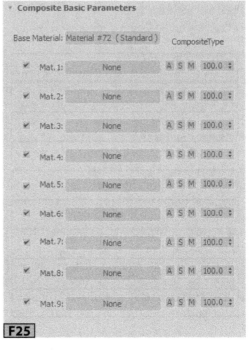

F25

Tip: Composite Material v Composite Map
*If you want to achieve a result by combining maps instead of combining materials, use the **Composite** map that provides greater control.*

Note: Overloaded compositing
*For additive and subtractive compositing, the amount can range from **0** to **200**. When the amount is greater than **100**, the compositing is overloaded. As a result, the transparent area of the material becomes more opaque.*

Morpher Material
The **Morpher** material is used with the **Morpher** modifier. For example, when a character raises his eyebrows, you can use this material to display wrinkles on his forehead. You can blend the materials the same way you morph the geometry using the channel spinners of the **Morpher** modifier.

Multi/Sub-Object Material
The **Multi/Sub-Object** material allows you to assign materials at the sub-object level. The number field [see Figure F26] shows the number of sub-materials contained in the **Multi/Sub-Object** material. You can use the **Set Number** button to set the number of sub-materials that make up the material. The **Add** button allows you to a new sub-material to the list. Use the **Delete** button to remove currently chosen sub-material from the list. The **ID, Name**, and **Sub-Material** controls allow you to sort the list based on the material id, name, and sub-material, respectively.

To assign materials to the sub-objects, select the object and assign the **Multi/sub-Object** material to it. Apply a **Mesh Select** modifier to the object. Activate the **Face**

F26

sub-object level. Now, select the faces to which you will assign the material. Apply a **Material Modifier** and then set the material ID value to the number of the sub-material you need to assign.

Shellac Material

Shellac material allows you to mix two materials by superimposing one over the other. The superimposed material is known as the **Shellac** material. The **Base Material** control [Figure F27] lets you choose or edit the base sub-material. The **Shellac Material** control lets you choose or edit the **Shellac** material. The **Shellac Color Blend** control adjusts the amount of color mixing. The default value for this control is **O**. Hence, the **Shellac** material has

no effect on the surface. There is no upper limit for this control. Higher values overload the colors of the **Shellac** material. You can also animate this parameter.

Top/Bottom Material

This material lets you assign two different materials to the top and bottom portions of an object. You can also blend the two materials. The top faces of an object are those faces whose normals point up. The bottom faces have the normals down. You can control the boundary between the top and bottom using the controls available in the **Coordinates** group [see Figure F28].

The **World** option lets you specify the direction according to the world coordinates of the scene. If you rotate the object, the boundary between the top and bottom faces remains in place. The **Local** option allows you to control the direction using the local coordinate system.

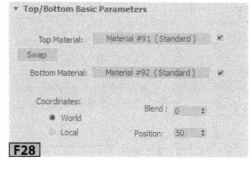

You can specify the top and bottom materials using the **Top** and **Bottom** controls, respectively. The **Swap** button allows you to swap the material. You can blend the edge between the top and bottom materials using the **Blend** control. The value for this control ranges from **O** to **1**. If you set **Blend** to **O**, there will be a sharp line between the top and bottom materials. At **100**, the two materials tint each other.

The **Position** control allows you to specify the location where the division between the two materials will occur. The value for this control ranges from **O** to **1**. If you set **Position** to **O**, only top material will be displayed. At **100**, only bottom material will be displayed.

Matte/Shadow Material

The **Matte/Shadow** material is used to make whole objects or any set of faces into matte objects. The matte objects reveal the background color or the environment map. A matte object is invisible but it blocks any geometry behind it however it does not block the background. The matte objects can also receive shadows. The shadows cast on the matte object are applied to the alpha channel. To properly generate shadows on a matte object, turn off **Opaque Alpha** and then turn on **Affect Alpha**.

Ink 'n Paint Material

The **Ink 'n Paint** material is used to create cartoons effects. This material produces shading with inked borders.

DirectX Shader Material

It is a special material that allows you to shade objects in the viewport using DirectX (Direct3D) shaders. When you use this material, materials in the viewport more accurately represent how they will look on some other software or hardware device.

Tip: Quicksilver hardware renderer
*You can use the **Quicksilver hardware renderer** to render **DirectX Shader** materials.*

XRef Material

This material lets you use a material applied to an object in another 3ds Max scene file. This material is typically used with the XRef objects. You can also use the **Override Material** rollout to assign a local material to the XRef'd object.

Physical Material

Physical material allows you to model shading effects of the real-world materials with ease. This material is the layered material that gives you ability to efficiently use the physically-based workflows. This material is compatible with **ART** and **mental ray** renderers.

General/Scanline Maps

Maps allow you to improve the appearance of the materials. They also help you to enhance the realism of the materials. You can use maps in a variety of ways, you can use them to create environments, to create image planes for modeling, to create projections from light, and so forth. You can use **Material/Map Browser** to load a map or create a map of a particular type. A map can be used to design different elements of a material such as reflection, refraction, bump, and so forth.

Maps and Mapping Coordinates

When you apply a map to any object, the object must have mapping coordinates applied. These coordinates are specified in terms of UVW axes local to the object. Most of the objects in 3ds Max have the **Generate Mapping Coordinates** option. When on, 3ds Max generates default mapping coordinates.

UVW Mapping Coordinate Channels

Each object in 3ds Max can have **99** UVW mapping coordinates. The default mapping is always assigned the number **1**. The **UVW Map** modifier can send coordinates to any of these **99** channels.

3ds Max gives you ability to generate the mapping coordinates in different ways:

- The **Generate Mapping Coords** option is available for most of the primitives. This option provides a projection appropriate to the shape of the object type.
- Apply the **Unwrap UVW** modifier. This modifier comes with some useful tools that you can use to edit mapping coordinates.
- Apply the **UVW Map** modifier. This modifier allows you to set a projection type from several projection types it provides.

Here's the quick rundown to the projection types:

- **Box projection:** It places a duplicate of the map image on each of the six sides of a box.

- **Cylindrical projection:** This wraps the image around the sides of the object. The duplicate images are also projected onto the end caps.

- **Spherical projection:** This projection type wraps the map image around a sphere and gather the image at the top and bottom.

- **Shrink-wrap projection:** This type is like the spherical projection but creates one singularity instead of two.

- Use special mapping coordinates. For example, the **Loft** object provides built-in mapping coordinates.
- Use a **Surface Mapper** modifier. This modifier uses a map assigned to a NURBS surface and projects it onto the object(s).

Here's quick rundown to the cases when you can apply a map and you don't need mapping coordinates:

- Reflection, Refraction, and Environment maps.
- 3D Procedural maps: **Noise** and **Marble**.
- Face-mapped materials.

Tip: UVW Remove utility
*The **UVW Remove** utility removes mapping coordinates or materials from the currently selected objects. The path to the utility is as follows: **Utilities** panel | **Utilities** rollout | **More** button | **Utilities** dialog | **UVW Remove**. You can also remove material from objects using the **UVW Remove** utility.*

Real-World Mapping
The real-world mapping is an alternative mapping method that you can use in 3ds Max. This type of mapping considers the correct scaling of the texture mapped materials applied to the geometry in the scene.

Note: Autodesk Materials
Autodesk materials require you to use the real-world mapping.

In order to apply the real-world mapping correctly, two requirements must be met. First, the correct style of UV texture coordinates must be assigned to the geometry. In other words, the size of the UV space should correspond to the size of the geometry. To address this issue, the **Real-World Map Size** switch is added to the many rollouts in 3ds Max [see Figure F29].

The second requirement is available in the **Coordinates** rollout of **Material Editor**, the **Use Real-World Scale** switch. When this switch is on, **U/V** changes to **Width/Height** and **Tiling** changes to **Size** [see Figure F30].

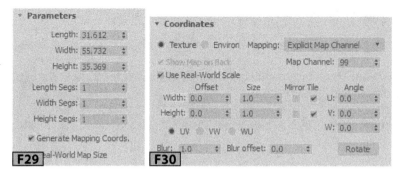

Note: Real-world Mapping

The real-world mapping is off in 3ds Max, by default.

Tip: Real-World Map Size check box

You can turn on **Real-World Map Size** *by default from the* **Preferences** *dialog by using the* **Use Real-World Texture Coordinates** *switch. This option is available in the* **Texture Coordinates** *section of the* **General** *panel.*

Output Rollout

The options in this rollout [see Figure F31] are responsible for setting the internal parameters of a map. These options can be used to determine the rendered appearance of the map. Most of the controls on this rollout are for the color output.

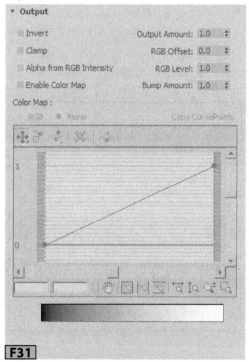

Note: Output Rollout
These controls do not affect the bump maps except the Invert toggle, which reverses the direction of the bumps and bump amount.

2D Maps

The 2D maps are two-dimensional images that are mapped to the surface of the geometric objects. You can also use them to create environment maps. The **Bitmap** is the simplest type 2D maps. 3ds Max also allows you to create 2D maps procedurally.

Coordinates Rollout

The **Coordinates** rollout shown in Figure F30 allows you to adjust coordinate parameters to move a map relative to the surface of the object. This rollout also allows you to set tiling and mirroring of the texture pattern. The repetition of the texture pattern on the surface of an object is known as tiling. The mirroring is a form of tiling in which 3ds Max repeats the map and then flips the repeated map.

In this rollout, there are two options that you can use to control the mapping type. These options are **Texture** and **Environ**. The **Texture** type applies texture as a map to the surface. The **Environ** type uses map as an environment map. For both of these options, you can select the types of coordinates from the **Mapping** drop-down.

Here's the list of options available in the **Mapping** drop-down:

- **Explicit Map Channel:** It uses any map channel from **1** to **99**. When you select this option, **Map Channel** becomes active.
- **Vertex Color Channel:** This option uses assigned vertex colors as a channel.
- **Planar from Object XYZ:** This option uses planar mapping based on the object's local coordinates.
- **Planar from World XYZ:** This option uses planar mapping based on the scene's world coordinates.
- **Spherical Environment/Cylindrical Environment/Shrink-wrap Environment:** These options project the map into the scene as if it were mapped to an invisible object in the background.
- **Screen:** This option projects a map as a flat backdrop in the scene.

Noise Rollout

You can add a random noise to the appearance of the material using the parameters available in this rollout [see Figure F32]. These parameters modify the mapping of pixels by applying a fractal noise function.

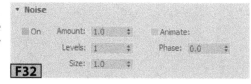

Bitmap

This map is the simplest type of map available in 3ds Max. This map is useful for creating many type of materials from wood to skin. If you want to create an animated material, you can use an animation or video file with this map. When you select this map, the **Select Bitmap Image File** dialog opens. Navigate to the location where the bitmap file is stored and then click **Open** to select the file.

Tip: Bitmap and Windows Explorer
*You can also create a bitmap node by dragging a supported bitmap file from **Windows Explorer** to **Slate Material Editor**.*

Tip: Viewport Canvas

*The **Viewport Canvas** feature allows you create a bitmap on the fly by painting directly onto the surface of the object. To open the canvas, choose **Viewport Canvas** from the **Tools** menu.*

Checker Map

This map is a procedural texture that applies a two-color checkerboard pattern [see Figure F33]. The default colors used to produce the pattern are black and white. You can also change these colors with map and it's true for all color components of the other maps.

Camera Map Per Pixel Map

This map allows you to project a map from the direction of a particular camera. It is useful when you are working on a matte painting. Figure F34 shows the **Marble** map projected on the teapot using the camera [see Figure F35]. Figure F36 shows the node network.

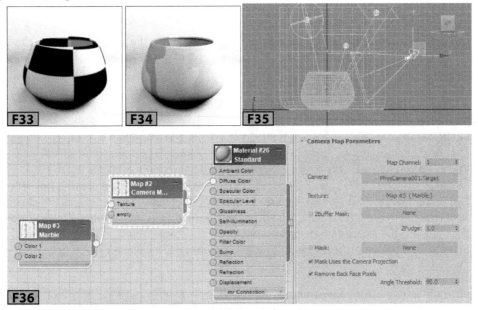

Note: Two maps with the sane name

If a map with the same name exists in two places, only one map is loaded to save the loading time. If you have two maps with different contents but with the same name, only the first map encountered by 3ds Max appears in the scene.

Tip: Swapping Colors

*You can swap colors by dragging one color swatch over another and then choosing **Swap** from the popup menu.*

Warning: Camera Map Per Pixel Map

This map cannot be used with the animated objects or animated textures.

Gradient Map

This map type allows you to create a gradient that shades from one color to another. Figure F37 shows the shift from one color to another. The red, green, and blue colors are used for the gradient. Figure F38 shows the result when the fractal noise is applied to the gradient. Figure F39 shows the node network.

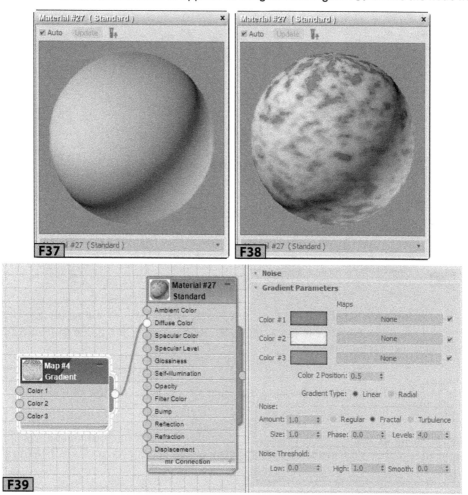

Gradient Ramp Map

This map is similar to the **Gradient** map. Like the **Gradient** map, it shades from one color to another, however, you can use any number of colors [see Figure F40]. Also, you have additional controls to create a complex customized ramp. Figure F41 shows the node network used to produce the result shown in Figure F40.

Normal Bump Map

This map allows you to connect a texture-baked normal map to a material. Figure F42 shows the bump on the surface created using the **Normal Bump** map. Figure F43 shows the node network.

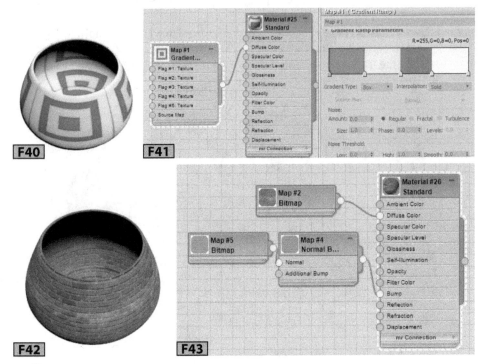

F40

F41

F42

F43

Substance Map

This map is used with the **Substance** parametric textures. These textures are resolution-independent 2D textures and use less memory. Therefore, they are useful for exporting to the game engines via the **Algorithmic Substance Air** middleware.

Swirl Map

This map is 2D procedural map that can be used to simulate swirls [see Figure F44].

Tiles Map

You can use this map to create a brick or stacked tiling of colors or maps. A number of commonly used architectural brick patterns are available with this map. Figure F45 shows render with the **English Bond** type applied.

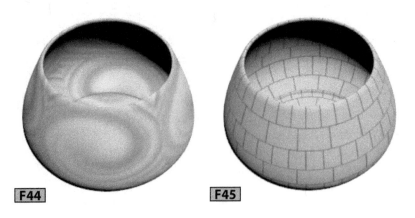

F44

F45

Vector Map

Using this map, you can apply a vector-based graphics, including animation as textures. You can also use **AutoCAD Pattern** (PAT) files, **Adobe Illustrator** (AI) files, **Portable Document** (PDF) files, and **Scalable Vector Graphics** (SVG) files [see Figure 46].

Vector Displacement Map

This map allows you to displace the meshes in three directions whereas the traditional method permits displacement only along the surface normals.

3D Maps

3D maps are patterns generated by 3ds Max in 3D space. Let's have a look at various 3D maps.

Cellular Map

You can use this map to generate a variety of visual effects such as mosaic tiling, pebbled surfaces, and even ocean surfaces [see Figure F47].

Dent Map

This map generates a procedural map using a fractal noise algorithm. The effect that this produces depends on the map type chosen.

Falloff Map

The **Falloff** map generates a value from white to black based on the angular falloff of the face normals. Figure F48 shows the **Falloff** map applied to the geometry with the **Falloff** type set to **Fresnel**.

F46

F47

F48

Marble Map

You can use this map to create a marble texture with the colored veins against [see Figure F49] a color background.

Noise Map

This map allows to create a noise map that creates the random perturbation of a surface based on the interaction of two colors or materials. Figure F50 shows the **Noise** map with the **Noise Type** set to **Fractal**.

Particle Age Map

This map is used with the particle systems. This map changes the color of the particles based on their age.

Particle MBlur Map

This map can be used to alter the opacity of the leading and trailing ends of particles based on their rate of motion.

Perlin Marble Map

This map is like the **Marble** map. However, it generates a marble pattern using the **Perlin Turbulence** algorithm.

Smoke Map

You can use this map [see Figure F51] to create animated opacity maps to simulate the effects of smoke in a beam of light, or other cloudy, flowing effects.

Speckle Map

This map [see Figure F52] can be used to create granite-like and other patterned surfaces.

Splat Map

This map can be used to create patterns similar to the spattered paint [see Figure F53].

Stucco Map

You can use this map [see Figure F54] as a bump to create the effect like a stuccoed surface.

Waves Map

You can use this map as both bump or diffuse map [see Figure F55]. This map is used to create watery or wavy effects.

Wood Map

This map creates a wavy grain like wood pattern [see Figure F56]. You can control the direction, thickness, and complexity of the grain.

Compositor Maps

These maps are specifically designed for compositing colors and maps. Let's have a look at these maps.

Composite Map

You can use this map to layer other maps atop each other using the alpha channel and other methods.

Mask Map

This map can be used to view one material through another on the surface.

Mix Map

With this map, you can combine two colors or materials on a single side of the surface. You can also animate the **Mix Amount** parameter to control how two maps are blended together over time.

RGB Multiply Map

This map combines two maps by multiplying their RGB values. This map is generally used as a **Bump** map.

Color Modifiers Maps

These maps change the color of the pixels in a material. Let's have a look:

Color Correction Map

This map is allows you to modify color of a map using various tools. This map uses a stack-based method.

Output Map

You can use this map to apply output settings to the procedural maps such as **Checker** or **Marble**. These maps don't have the output settings.

RGB Tint Map

This map adjusts the three color channels in an image.

Vertex Color Map

In 3ds Max, you can assign vertex colors using the **VertexPaint** modifier, the **Assign Vertex Colors** utility, or the vertex controls for an editable mesh, editable patch, or editable poly. This map makes any vertex coloring applied to an object available for rendering.

Reflection and Refraction Maps

These maps are used to create reflections and refractions. Here's is a quick rundown.

Flat Mirror Map

This map produces a material that reflects surroundings when it is applied to the co-planer faces. It is assigned to the **Reflection** map of the material.

Raytrace Map

This map allows you to create fully raytraced reflections and refractions. The reflections/refractions generated by this map are more accurate than the **Reflect/Refract** map.

Reflect/Refract Map

You can use this map to create a reflective or refractive surface. To create reflection, assign this map type to the reflection map. To create refraction, apply it to the **Refraction** map.

Thin Wall Refraction Map

This map can be used to simulate a surface as if it part of a surface through a plate of glass.

Other Maps

Here's is a quick rundown.

Shape Map

You can use this map to create resolution independent graphical textures that you can animate. This map uses splines to apply textures to the selected object. The results can be fully animated. You can set outlines, fill colors as well as the map boundaries. You can change the shape of the spline even after applying it to the object in the scene. Also, all adjustment to the shape can be keyframed as a result you can animate the textures. The functioning of this map is demonstrated in an hands-on exercise later in the unit.

Text Map

Like splines, you can also create textures using text. You can create creative textures using the **Text** map and all adjustments can be animated. The functioning of this map is demonstrated in an hands-on exercise later in the unit.

TextureObjMask

This texture map allows you to control the textures using a primitive control object [plane, box, or sphere]. You can use the box or sphere primitive to control inside/outside color. The plan primitive allows you to control above/below color. The functioning of this map is demonstrated in an hands-on exercise later in the unit.

Color Map

This map allows you to create solid color swatches and bitmaps. You can easily create and instance solid color swatches that allows you to maintain consistency and accuracy of color choices. You can also use a bitmap as an input and adjust gamma and gain.

Combustion

You can use this map to interactively create maps using Autodesk Combustion and 3ds Max simultaneously. When you paint a map in combustion the material automatically updated in 3ds Max [material editor and shaded viewports].

Caution: Combustion

This map works only if Autodesk Combustion is installed on your system. 3ds Max is only available for Windows, as a result, you can not use this map on a Macintosh system.

Map Output Selector

This map is used with the multi-output map such as Substance. It tells 3ds Max which output to use. This map is automatically inserted when you assign an output of multi-output Substance map to input of a material.

MultiTile

This texture allows you to implement support for UDIM, Z-Brush, and Mudbox compatible multi-tile textures. ZBrush is the default value.

Hands-on Exercises

From the **File** menu, choose **Set Project Folder** to open the **Browse for Folder** dialog. Navigate to the folder where you want to save the files and then click **Make New Folder**. Create the new folder with the name **unit-mt3** and click **OK** to create the project directory.

Exercise 1: Creating the Gold Material

In this exercise, we are going to create the gold material.

The following table summarizes the exercise.

Table E1: Creating the gold material	
Topics in this section:	• Getting Ready • Creating the Gold Material
Skill Level	Beginner
Project Folder	**unit-mt3**
Start File	**umt3-hoe1-1to10-start.max**
Final Exercise File	**umt3-hoe1-end.max**
Time to Complete	10 Minutes

Getting Ready

Open the **umt3-hoe1-1to10-start.max** file in 3ds Max.

Creating the Gold Material

Press M to open **Slate Material Editor**. On **Material/Map Browser | Materials | General** rollout, drag the **Standard** material to the active view. Rename the material as **goldMat**. Apply the material to **geo1**, **geo2**, and **geo3**. Save the scene as **umt3-hoe1-end.max**. On the **Parameter Editor | goldMat | Shader Basic Parameters** rollout, choose **Multi-Layer** from the drop-down. On the **Multi-Layer Basic Parameters** rollout, set **Diffuse** to **RGB [148, 70, 0]** and then set **Diffuse Level** to **25**. Render the scene [see Figure E1].

Now, we will add specularity and reflection to add the detail. On the **First Specular Layer** section, set **Color** to **RGB [247, 227, 10]**. Set **Level** to **114**, **Glossiness** to **32**, **Anisotropy** to **82**, and **Orientation** to **90**.

On the **Second Specular Layer** section, set **Color** to **RGB [192, 77, 8]**. Set **Level** to **114**, **Glossiness** to **32**, **Anisotropy** to **82**, and **Orientation** to **90**. On the **Maps** rollout, click **Reflection** map button.

On **Material/Map Browser** that appears, double-click **Falloff**. On **Parameter Editor | Falloff | Falloff Parameters** rollout, click the **Swap Colors/Maps** button. Also, set **Falloff Type** to **Fresnel**. Click white swatch map button and then on **Material/Map Browser** that appears, double-click **Raytrace** in the **Maps | General** rollout.

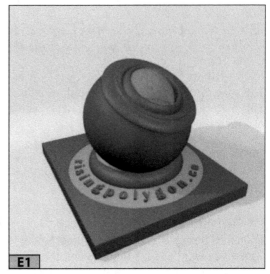
E1

On the **Parameter Editor | Raytrace | Raytracer Parameters** rollout, select **Reflection** from the **Trace Mode** section. Render the scene [see Figure E2].

On the **Falloff | Mix Curve** rollout, RMB click on the first point and then choose **Bezier-Corner** from the contextual menu [see Figure E3].

Similarly, convert second point to **Bezier-Corner** and change the shape of the curve as shown in Figure E4. Now, Render the scene to view the final result [see Figure E5].

E2

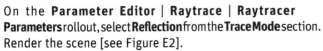
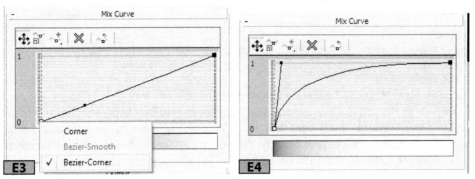
E3

E4

E5

Exercise 2: Creating the Copper Material

In this exercise, we are going to create the copper material. The following table summarizes the exercise.

Table E2: Creating the copper material	
Topics in this section:	• Getting Ready • Creating the Copper Material
Skill Level	Beginner
Project Folder	**unit-mt3**
Start File	**umt3-hoe1-end.max**
Final Exercise File	**umt3-hoe2-end.max**
Time to Complete	10 Minutes

Getting Ready

Make sure the **umt3-hoe1-end.max** file that you created in Hands-on Exercise 1 is open in 3ds Max.

Creating the Copper Material

Press M to open **Slate Material Editor**, if not already open. Create a copy of the **goldMat** node by shift dragging it [see Figure E1]. Rename the node as **copperMat** and then apply it to **geo1, geo2,** and **geo3**. Save the scene as **umt3-hoe2-end.max**. On the **Multi-Layer Basic Parameters** rollout, set **Diffuse** to **RGB [88, 28, 9]**. On the **First Specular Layer section**, set **Color** to **RGB [177, 75, 44]**. On the **Second Specular Layer section**, set **Color** to **RGB [255, 123, 82]**. Take the render [see Figure E2].

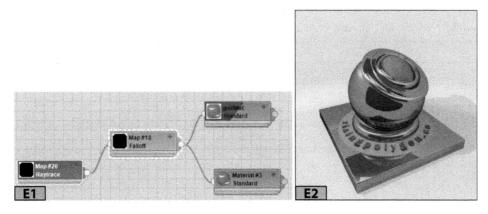

E1

E2

Exercise 3: Creating the Brass Material

In this exercise, we are going to create the brass material. The following table summarizes the exercise.

Table E3: Creating the brass material	
Topics in this section:	• Getting Ready • Creating the Brass Material
Skill Level	Beginner
Project Folder	**unit-mt3**
Start File	**umt3-hoe2-end.max**
Final Exercise File	**umt3-hoe3-end.max**
Time to Complete	10 Minutes

Getting Ready

Make sure the **umt3-hoe2-end.max** file that you created in Hands-on Exercise 2 is open in 3ds Max.

Creating the Brass Material

Press M to open **Slate Material Editor**, if not already open. Create a copy of the **copperMat** node by **Shift** dragging it. Rename the node as **brassMat** and then apply it to **geo1**, **geo2**, and **geo3**.

E1

On the **Multi-Layer Basic Parameters** rollout, set **Diffuse** to **RGB [49, 38, 14]**. On the **First Specular Layer** section, set **Color** to **RGB [212, 154, 30]**. On the **Second Specular Layer** section, set **Color** to **RGB [174, 98, 61]**. Render the scene [see Figure E1] and then save the file with the name **umt3-hoe3-end.max**.

Exercise 4: Creating the Chrome Material

In this exercise, we are going to create the chrome material.

The following table summarizes the exercise.

Table E4: Creating the chrome material	
Topics in this section:	• Getting Ready • Creating the Chrome Material
Skill Level	Beginner
Project Folder	**unit-mt3**
Start File	**umt3-hoe1-1to10-start.max**
Final Exercise File	**umt3-hoes4-end.max**
Time to Complete	10 Minutes

Getting Ready
Make sure the **hoes1-1to13-start.max** is open in 3ds Max.

Creating the Chrome Material

Load **umt3-hoe1-1to10-start.max** in 3ds Max. Press **M** to open **Slate Material Editor**. On the **Material/Map/Browser | Materials | General** rollout, drag the **Standard** material to the active view. Rename the material as **chromeMat**. Apply the material to **geo1**, **geo2**, and **geo3**. Save the scene as **umt3-hoes4-end.max**.

On the **Parameter Editor | chromeMat | Blinn Basic Parameters** rollout, click the **Diffuse** color swatch. On the **Color Selector : Diffuse Color** dialog, set **Value** to **12** and click **OK**. On the **Specular Highlights** section, set **Specular Level** to **150** and **Glossiness** to **80**.

On the **Maps** rollout, set **Reflection** to **90** and then click the **Reflection** map button. On **Material Map Browser** that appears, double-click **Raytrace**. On the **Raytrace** map | **Raytracer Parameters | Background** section, click **None**.

On **Material/Map Browser** that appears, double-click **Bitmap**. In the **Select Bitmap Image File** dialog that appears, select **refMap.jpeg**. Render the scene [see Figure E1].

E1

Exercise 5: Creating the Brushed Aluminum Material

In this exercise, we are going to create the brushed aluminum material using Photoshop and 3ds Max. The following table summarizes the exercise.

Table E5: Creating the brushed aluminum material	
Topics in this section:	• Getting Ready • Creating the Brushed Aluminum Material
Skill Level	Beginner
Project Folder	**unit-mt3**
Start File	**umt3-hoe1-1to10-start.max**
Final Exercise File	**umt3-hoe5-end.max**
Time to Complete	15 Minutes

Getting Ready

Make sure the **umt3-hoe1-1to10-start.max** is open in 3ds Max.

Creating the Brushed Aluminum Material

Start Photoshop. Create a **1000 x 1000 px** document and fill it with **50%** gray color. Choose **Noise | Add Noise** from the **Filter** menu and then set the parameters as shown in Figure E1 and then click **OK**. Choose **Blur | Motion Blur** from the **Filter** menu and then set the parameters as shown in Figure E2 and then click **OK**. Choose **Adjustments | Brightness\Contrast** from the **Image** menu and then set the parameters as shown in Figure E3 and then click **OK**. Save the document as **scratch.jpg**.

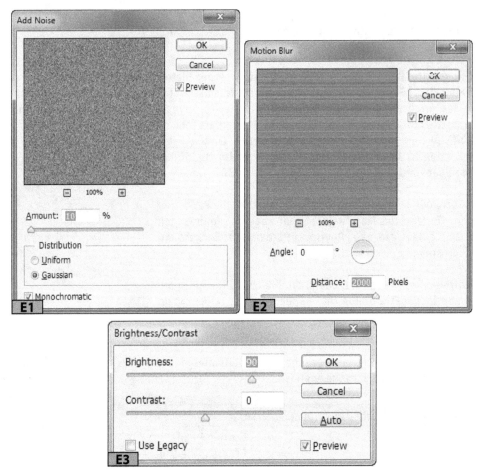

Load **umt3-hoe1-1to10-start.max** in 3ds Max, if not already loaded. Press **M** to open **Slate Material Editor**. On the **Material/Map Browser | Materials | General** rollout, drag the **Standard** material to the active view. Rename the material as **balMat**. Apply the material to **geo1**, **geo2**, and **geo3**.

On the **Parameter Editor | balMat | Shader Basic Parameters** rollout, choose **Oren-Nayar-Blinn** from the drop-down. On the **Parameter Editor | balMat | Oren-Nayar-Blinn Basic Parameters** rollout, click **Ambient** color swatch. On the **Color Selector : Ambient Color** dialog, set **Value** to **84** and click **OK**. Unlock the **Ambient** and **Diffuse** components of the material.

Click the **Diffuse** map button and then on **Material/Map Browser** that appears, double-click **Mix**. On the **Parameter Editor | Mix map**, set **Color 1** to the value **127** and assign **scratch.jpg** to **Color 2** using the **Bitmap** map. Set **Mix Amount** to **72%**. On the **balMat | Oren-Nayar-Blinn Basic Parameters** rollout | **Advanced Diffuse** section, set **Diffuse Level** to **81**, and **Roughness** to **80**. Now, render the scene [see Figure E4]. On the **Parameter Editor | balMat | Oren-Nayar-Blinn Basic Parameters** rollout | **Specular Highlight** section, set **Specular Level** to **156**, **Glossiness** to **13**, and **Soften** to **0.48**. Now, render the scene [see Figure E5]. On the **Parameter Editor | scratch.jpg | Output** rollout, set **Output Amount** to **0.6**. Render the scene [see Figure E6]. Save the file as **umt3-hoe5-end.max**.

Exercise 6: Creating the Denim Fabric Material

In this exercise, we are going to create the denim fabric material using Photoshop and 3ds Max. The following table summarizes the exercise.

Table E6: Creating the denim fabric material	
Topics in this section:	• Getting Ready • Creating the Denim Fabric Material
Skill Level	Beginner
Project Folder	**unit-mt3**
Start File	**umt3-hoe1-1to10-start.max**
Final Exercise File	**umt3-hoe6-end.max**
Time to Complete	15 Minutes

Getting Ready

Make sure the **umt3-hoe1-1to10-start.max** is open in 3ds Max.

Creating the Denim Fabric Material

Start Photoshop. Create a **1000 x 1000 px** document and fill it with **RGB [41, 67, 102]** color. Create a new layer and fill it with **50%** gray. Press **D** to switch to the default colors. Choose **Filter Gallery| Sketch | Halftone Pattern** from the **Filter** menu and then set the parameters as shown in Figure E1 and then click **OK**. Choose **Pixelate | Mezzotint** from the **Filter** menu and then set the parameters as shown in Figure E2 and then click **OK**.

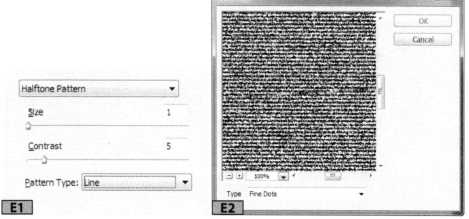

Duplicate the layer and rotate and scale the duplicate layer [see Figure E3]. Choose **Blur | Gaussian Blur** from the **Filter** menu and then apply a blur of radius **1**. Set blending mode to **Multiply**. Also, set the blending mode of the middle layer [Layer 1] to **Softlight** [Figure E4]. Save the file as **denimFebric.jpg**.

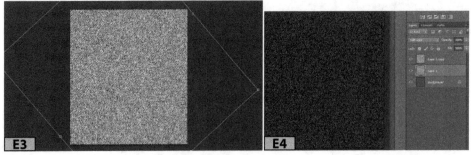

Choose **Flatten Image** from the **Layer** menu to flatten the image. Now, press **Ctrl+Shift+U** to desaturate the image and then save it as **denimFebricBump.jpg**. In 3ds Max, press **M** to open **Slate Material Editor**. On the **Material/Map Browser | Materials | Scanline** rollout, drag the **Standard** material to the active view. Rename the material as **denimMat**. Apply the material to **geo1**, **geo2**, and **geo3**.

Save the scene as **umt3-hoe6-end.max**. On the **Parameter Editor | denimMat | Shader Basic Parameters** rollout, choose **Oren-Nayar-Blinn** from the drop-down. On the **Parameter Editor | denimMat | Oren-Nayar-Blinn Basic Parameters** rollout, click **Ambient** color swatch.

On the **Color Selector : Ambient Color** dialog, set **RGB** to **50**, **53**, and **57** and click **OK**. Unlock the **Ambient** and **Diffuse** components of the material. Click the **Diffuse** map button and then on **Material Map Browser** that appears, double-click **Bitmap**. Assign **denimFebric.jpg**. On the **denimMat | Oren-Nayar-Blinn Basic Parameters** rollout | **Advanced Diffuse** section, set **Diffuse Level** to **250**, and **Roughness** to **75**. Now, render the scene [see Figure E5].

On the **Parameter Editor | denimMat | Oren-Nayar-Blinn Basic Parameters** rollout | **Specular Highlight** section, set **Specular Level** to **7**, and **Glossiness** to **10**. Render the scene [see Figure E6]. On the **Maps** rollout, ensure **Bump** is set to **30%** and then click **Bump** map button.

On **Material/Map Browser** that appears, double-click **Bitmap**. On the **Select Bitmap Image File** dialog that appears, select **denimFebricBump.jpg**. Take a test render [see Figure E7].

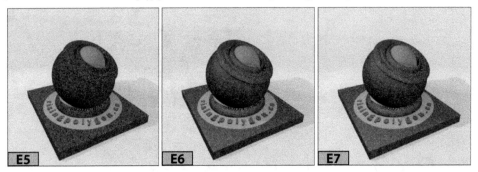

Exercise 7: Creating the Microscopic Material

In this exercise, we're going to create a microscopic material [see Figure E1]. The following material(s) and map(s) are used in this exercise: **Standard**, **Mix**, **Falloff**, and **Noise**.

The following table summarizes the exercise.

Table E7: Creating the microscopic material	
Topics in this section:	• Getting Ready • Creating the Microscopic Material
Skill Level	Beginner
Project Folder	**unit-mt3**
Start File	**umt3-hoe7-start.max**
Final Exercise File	**umt3-hoe7-end.max**
Time to Complete	15 Minutes

Getting Ready

Make sure the **umt3-hoe7-start.max** is open in 3ds Max.

Creating the Microscopic Material

Press **M** to open **Slate Material Editor** and then create a new **Standard** material and assign it to the **sphGeo** in the scene. Rename the material as **msMat**. Connect a **Falloff** map to the **msMat's Diffuse** port. On the **Parameter Editor | Falloff** map | **Falloff Parameters** rollout | **Front:Side** section, set first color swatch to **RGB [20, 20, 20]** and second color swatch to white. Set **Falloff Type** to **Perpendicular/Parallel**. Ensure **Falloff Direction** is set to **Viewing Direction (Camera Z-Axis)** [see Figure E2]. Also, set the **Mix Curve** to as shown in Figure E3.

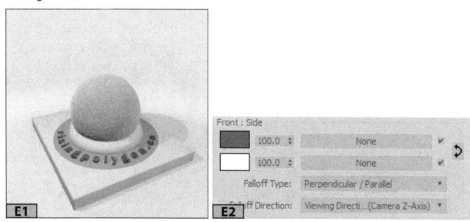

Now, you will create two **Noise** maps and mix them using the **Mix** map. Connect a **Mix** map to the **msMat's Bump** port. On the **Parameter Editor | Mix** map | **Mix Parameters** rollout, set **Mix Amount** to **37.8**. On the **Slate Material Editor**, connect two **Noise** maps, one each to the **Color 1** and **Color 2** ports. For the **Color 1 | Noise** map use the settings shown in Figure E4. Figure E5 shows the **Noise** map settings connected to **Color 2**. Figure E6 shows the node network.

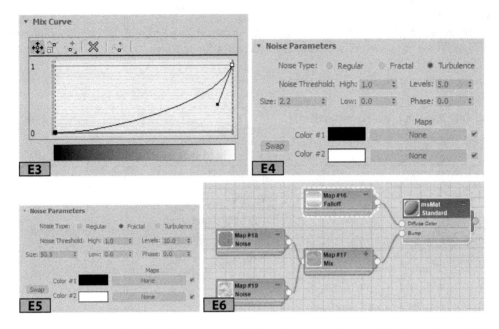

Now, render the scene. Notice that the output is little bit on the darker side. To address this, on the **Parameter Editor** | **Falloff** map | **Falloff Parameters** rollout | **Front:Side** section, set first color swatch to **RGB [80, 80, 80]**. Render the scene [see Figure E1].

Exercise 8: Creating Material for a Volleyball

Here, we are going to apply texture to a volleyball [see Figure E1]. Right image in Figure E1 shows the reference whereas the left image shows the rendered output. The following material(s) and map(s) are used in this exercise: **Multi/Sub-Object**, **Standard**, and **Noise**.

The following table summarizes the exercise.

Table E8: Creating material for a volleyball	
Topics in this section:	• Getting Ready • Creating Material for a Volleyball
Skill Level	Beginner
Project Folder	**unit-mt3**
Start File	**umt3-hoe8-start.max**
Final Exercise File	**umt3-hoe8-end.max**
Time to Complete	15 Minutes

Getting Ready
Make sure the **umt3-hoe8-start.max** is open in 3ds Max. Save the file as **umt3-hoe8-end.max**.

Creating Material for a Volleyball
Select the **VolleyBallGeo** in any viewport and then go to the **Modify** panel. On the **Selection** rollout, click **Element** and then select the elements that make the yellow part of the volleyball [see Figure E2]. See the right image in Figure E1 for reference.

On the **Modify panel | Polygon: Material IDs** rollout, set **ID** to **1** [see Figure E3]. Similarly, select the blue and white elements and assign them ID **2** and **3**, respectively. Press **M** to open **Slate Material Editor** and then create a new **Multi/Sub-object** material and assign it to the **VolleyBallGeo** in the scene. Rename the material as **vbMat**. On the **Parameter Editor | vbMat | Multi/Sub-Object Parameters** rollout, click **Set Number** and then set **Number of Materials** to **3** in the dialog that appears. Next, click **OK**. In **Slate Material Editor**, connect a **Standard** material to the port **1** of the **vbMat**. On the **Parameter Editor | Blinn Basic Parameter** rollout, set the **Diffuse** component to **RGB [242, 140, 8]**. On the **Specular Highlights** section, set **Specular Level** to **71** and **Glossiness** to **28**.

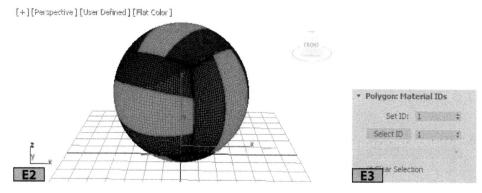

[+] [Perspective] [User Defined] [Flat Color]

E2

▼ Polygon: Material IDs

Set ID: 1

Select ID 1

Clear Selection

E3

Connect a **Noise** map to the **Bump** port of the **Standard** material. Set **Bump** to **2%**. On the **Parameter Editor | Noise map | Noise Parameters** rollout, set **Noise Type** to **Turbulence**, **Levels** to **9**, and **Size** to **0.5**. On **Slate Material Editor**, select the **Standard** material and **Noise** map. Now, create a copy of the selected nodes using **SHIFT**. Connect the new Standard material to the port **2** of the **vbMat**. Similarly, create another copy and connect it to port **3**. Figure E4 shows the node network. Set **Diffuse** components of the material connected to the port **2** and **3** to **RGB [11, 91, 229]** and **RGB [236, 236, 230]**, respectively. Now, Render the scene.

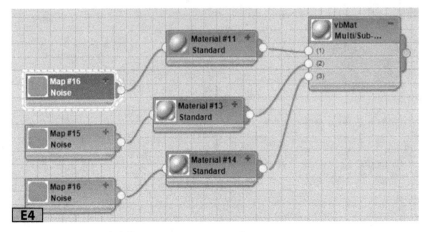

E4

Exercise 9: Creating Material for a Water Tunnel

Here, we are going to apply texture to a water tunnel [see Figure E1]. The following material(s) and map(s) are used in this exercise: **Raytrace**, **Standard**, **Mix**, and **Noise**.

E1

The following table summarizes the exercise.

Table E9: Creating material for a water tunnel	
Topics in this section:	• Getting Ready • Creating Material for a Water Tunnel
Skill Level	Beginner
Project Folder	**unit-mt3**
Start File	**umt3-hoes9-start.max**
Final Exercise File	**umt3-hoes9-end.max**
Time to Complete	15 Minutes

Getting Ready

Make sure the **umt3-hoes9-start.max** is open in 3ds Max.

Creating Material for a Water Tunnel

Press **M** to open **Slate Material Editor** and then create a new **Raytrace** material and assign it to the **waterGeo** in the scene. Rename the material as **waterMat**. On **Parameter Editor | Raytrace Basic Parameter** rollout, set **Diffuse** to **black**. Set **Transparency** to **RGB (146, 175, 223)**. Set **Reflect** to **RGB [178, 178, 178]**. On the **Specular Highlight** section, set **Specular Level** to **161** and **Glossiness** to **29**. Connect a **Noise** map to the **Bump** port of the **waterMat**. Use the default values for the **Noise** map. Render the scene [Figure E2].

On **Slate Material Editor**, create a new **Standard** material and assign it to the **caveGeo** in the scene. Rename the material as **caveMat**. Connect a **Mix** map to the **Diffuse** port of the **caveMat**. Connect a **Noise** map to the **Color 1** port of the **Mix** map. On the **Noise Parameters** rollout, set **Noise Type** to **Turbulence**, **Levels** to **10**, **Size** to **31.7**. Set **Color 1** to **RGB [132, 77, 6]** and **Color 2** to **RGB [154, 100, 79]**.

Connect a **Noise** map to the **Color 2** port of the **Mix** map. On the **Noise Parameters** rollout, set **Noise Type** to **Turbulence**, **Levels** to **10**, **Size** to **72**. Set **Color 1** to **RGB [212, 84, 45]** and **Color 2** to **RGB [181, 99, 54]**. On the **Parameter Editor | Mix Parameters** rollout, set **Mix Amount** to **40**. On the **Mixing curve** section, turn on the **Use Curve** switch and then set **Upper** to **0.6** and **Lower** to **0.53**. Render the [Figure E3].

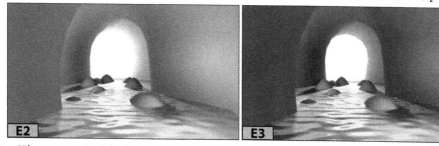

Connect a **Mix** map to the **Displacement** port of the **caveMat**. Set **Displacement** to **25%**. Connect a **Noise** map to the **Color 1** port of the **Mix** map. On the **Noise Parameters** rollout, set **Noise Type** to **Turbulence**, **Levels** to **8.4**, **Size** to **21.2**. Connect a **Noise** map to the **Color 2** port of the **Mix** map. On the **Noise Parameters** rollout, set **Noise Type** to **Turbulence**, **Levels** to **10**, **Size** to **81.5**. On the **Parameter Editor | Mix Parameters** rollout, set **Mix Amount** to **18.4**. Select **caveGeo** in the scene and then apply **Disp Approx** modifier to it. Render the scene [Figure E4]

Similarly, create a material for the **floorGeo**. If you want to see the values I have used, open **umt3-hoe9-end.max** and check the **floorMat** material.

Exercise 10: Creating Rusted Metal Texture

Let's now create a rusted metal texture [see Figure E1]. The following material(s) and map(s) are used in this exercise: **Standard**, **Composite**, **Bitmap**, **Color Correction**, and **Noise**. The following table summarizes the exercise.

Table E10: Creating rusted metal texture	
Topics in this section:	• Getting Ready • Creating Rusted Metal Texture
Skill Level	Beginner
Project Folder	**unit-mt3**
Start File	**umt3-hoe1-1to10-start.max**
Final Exercise File	**umt3-hoe10-end.max**
Time to Complete	15 Minutes

Getting Ready

Make sure the **umt3-hoe1-1to10-start.max** is open in 3ds Max. Save the file with the name **umt3-hoe10-end.max**.

Creating Rusted Metal Texture

Press **M** to open **Slate Material Editor**. In the **Material/Map Browser | Materials | General** rollout, double-click on **Standard** to add a **Standard** material to the active view. Rename the material as **rustMat** and apply it to **geo1**, **geo2**, and **geo3**.

Connect a **Composite** map to the **rustMap's Diffuse Color** port. Now, connect **rust.jpg** to the **Composite** map's **Layer 1** port [see Figure E2].

E1

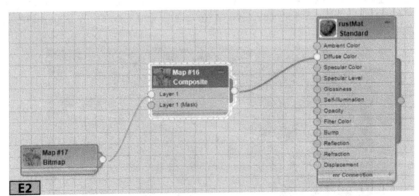

E2

On the **Parameter Editor | Composite** map | **Composite Layers | Layer 1** rollout, click **Add a New Layer** button to add a new layer [see Figure E3]. Notice that a new port with the name **Layer 2** has been added to the **Composite** map node in the active view. Connect **rustPaint.jpg** to the **Composite** map's **Layer 2** port. On the **Parameter Editor | Composite** map **| Composite Layers | Layer 2** rollout, set **Opacity** to **10%** and blend mode to **Color Dodge** [see Figure E4].

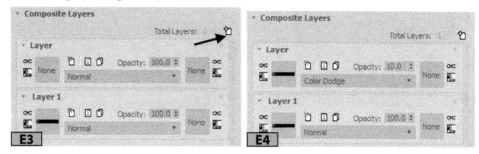

Now, render the scene [see Figure E5]. Connect **scratchesMask.jpg** to the **Composite** map's **Layer 2 (Mask)** port using a **Bitmap** map. Now, check the **Invert** checkbox from the **Bitmap's Output** rollout. Render the scene [see Figure E6]. On **Slate Material Editor's** active view, create copy of the **Bitmap** node connected to the **Composite** map's **Layer 2 (Mask)** node using **Shift**. Connect the duplicate node to the **Bump** node of **rustMat**. On the **Parameter Editor | rustMat | Maps** rollout, set bump map's strength to **10%** and then render the scene[see Figure E7].

Exercise 11: Shading an outdoor Scene

In this exercise, we are going to apply materials and textures to an outdoor scene [see Figure E1]. The following table summarizes the exercise.

Table E11: Shading an outdoor scene	
Topics in this section:	• Getting Ready • Shading the Scene
Skill Level	Intermediate
Project Folder	**unit-mt3**
Start File	**umt3-hoe11-start.max**
Final Exercise File	**umt3-hoe11-end.max**
Time to Complete	30 Minutes

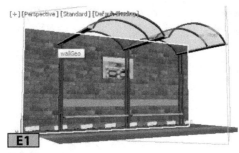 

Getting Ready

Make sure the **umt3-hoe11-start.max** is open in 3ds Max. Save the file with the name **umt3-hoe11-end.max**.

Shading the Scene

Select **wallGeo** from **Scene Explorer** and then press **M** to open **Slate Material Editor**. Drag **Standard** from the **Material/Map Browser | Maps | Scanline** rollout to **Active View**. Rename the material as **wallMat**. RMB click on the **wallMat** node and then choose **Assign Material to Selection**. Again, RMB click and then choose **Show Shaded Material in Viewport**.

In **Active View**, drag the **Diffuse Color** socket onto the empty area and release the mouse button. Choose **General | Bitmap** from the popup menu. In the **Select Bitmap Image File** dialog that opens, select **redBrick.png** and then click **Open** to make a connection between the **Diffuse Color** socket and texture. Double-click on the **Bitmap** node and then in the **Parameter Editor | Coordinates** rollout, set **U Tiling** and **V Tiling** to **4**. Similarly, connect the **Bump** socket to the **redBrickGray.png** and set **Tiling** to **4**.

Notice in the viewport the map is displayed on the wall [see the left image in Figure E2]. Ensure **wallGeo** is selected in **Scene Explorer** and then go to **Modify** panel and add the **UVW Map** modifier to the stack. Select the modifier's **Gizmo** and scale the texture so that the size of the bricks appear in right proportions [see the right image in Figure E2].

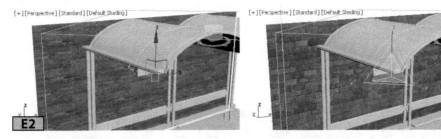

Select **floorGeo** from the **Scene Explorer** and then in **Slate Material Editor**, drag **Standard** from the **Material/Map Browser | Maps | General** rollout to **Active View**. Rename the material as **roadMat**. RMB click on the **roadMat** node and then choose **Assign Material to Selection**. Again, RMB click and then choose **Show Shaded Material in Viewport**. In **Active View**, drag the **Diffuse Color** socket onto the empty area and release the mouse button. Choose **General | Bitmap** from the popup menu. In the **Select Bitmap Image File** dialog that opens, select **road.jpg** and then click **Open** to make a connection between the **Diffuse Color** socket and texture. Notice in the viewport, the texture appears on the **floorGeo** [see Figure E3]. Now, we need to change the direction of the yellow line. We will do so by using the **UVW Map** modifier.

Ensure **floorGeo** is selected in **Scene Explorer** and then go to **Modify** panel and add the **UVW Map** modifier to the stack. Select the modifier's **Gizmo** and rotate it by **90** degrees by using the **Rotate** tool. You can also use the **Move** tool to position the texture on the geometry [see Figure E4].

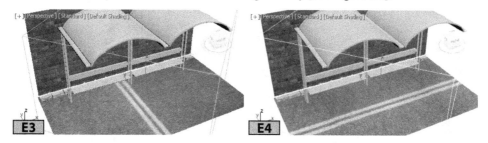

Now, we will apply the material to billboard. We will use the **Multi/Subobject** material. The ID **1** has been assigned to the screen component of the board whereas rest of the geometry is held by ID **2**. Select **billBoardGeo** from **Scene Explorer** and then add a **Multi/Subobject** node to **Active View**. Rename the material as **billboardMat**. In the **Parameter Editor**, click **Set Number**. Now, in the **Set Number of Materials** dialog, set **Number of Materials** field to **2** and click **OK**. RMB click on the **billboardMat** node and then choose **Assign Material to Selection**.

Drag the **1** socket to the empty area of the view and then choose **Materials | Scanline | Standard** from the popup menu. Connect the **Standard's** materials **Diffuse Color** socket to the **honda.jpg**. Connect another **Standard** material to the **2** socket of the **billboardMat**. In the **Parameter Editor | Blinn Basic Parameters rollout | Specular Highlight** group of the **Standard** material, set **Specular Level** and **Glossiness** to **92** and **33**, respectively. Also, set **Diffuse** color to **RGB [20, 20, and 20]**.

The material appears on the **billBoardGeo** in the viewport [see Figure E5]. You need to enable **Show Shaded Material in Viewport** for the two Standard materials. Create two **Standard** materials and assign dark gray and yellow colors to them. Now, apply these materials to alternate brick from the **brickGrp** group [see Figure E6].

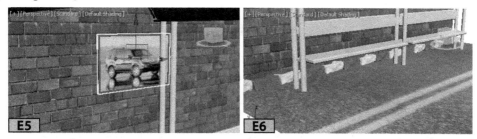

Now, create a chrome material as done in Exercise 4. Do not assign the **rcfMap.jpg** to the **Raytrace** map. In **Scene Explorer**, select **bsGeo11, bsGeo12, bsGeo15, bsGeo16, bsGeo18, bsGeo19, bsGeo20, bsGeo22, bsGeo23, bsGeo24, bsGeo26,** and **bsGeo27**. Assign chrome material to the selected objects [see Figure E7]. Also, assign chrome material to **bsGeo3**, and **bsGeo6**.

In **Scene Explorer**, select **bsGeo04, bsGeo05, bsGeo07,** and **bsGeo08**. Drag **Standard** from the **Material/Map Browser | Maps | General** rollout to **Active View**. Rename the material as **woodMat**. RMB click on the **woodMat** node and then choose **Assign Material to Selection**. Again, RMB click and then choose **Show**

Shaded Material in Viewport. In **Active View**, drag the **Diffuse Color** socket onto the empty area and release the mouse button. Choose **General | Wood** from the popup menu. In the **Parameter Editor | Wood | Wood Parameters** rollout, change **Color #2** to **RGB[106, 25, 0]**. The wood texture is displayed in the viewport [see Figure E8].

In **Scene Explorer**, select **bsGeo21**, and **bsGeo25** and then drag **Standard** from the **Material/Map Browser | Maps | General** rollout to **Active View**. Rename the material as **roofMat**. RMB click on the **roofMat** node and then choose **Assign Material to Selection**. Again, RMB click and then choose **Show Shaded Material in Viewport**. In the **Parameter Editor | roofMat | Blinn Basic Parameters** rollout, change **Diffuse** to **RGB[23, 241, 12]** and then set **Opacity** to **25**. Figure E9 shows the roof material in the viewport.

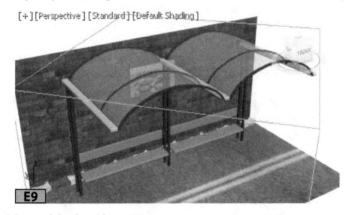

Exercise 12: Working with the ShapeMap

In this exercise, we will create a resolution independent map using the **ShapeMap**.

The following Table summarizes the exercise.

Table E12: Working with the ShapeMap	
Topics in this section:	• Getting Ready • Working with ShapeMap
Skill Level	Beginner
Project Folder	**unit-mt3**
Start File	**umt3-hoe12-start.max**
Final Exercise File	**umt3-hoe12-end.max**
Time to Complete	20 Minutes

Getting Ready

Open **umt3-hoe12-start.max** in 3ds Max.

Working with the ShapeMap

Press **M** to open **Slate Material Editor** and then from the **Material/Map Browser** | **General** | **Maps** rollout, drag **Standard** to the active view. Connect **ShapeMap** to the **Diffuse** slot of the material. Select the plane in the viewport. RMB click on the material node and then choose **Assign Material to Selection**. Again, RMB click and then choose **Show Shaded Material in Viewport**. Notice only standard logo is displayed in the viewport at this moment [see Figure E1].

On the **Parameter Editor** | **ShapeMap** | **Shape Parameters** rollout, click **None** and then click the apple logo spline in any viewport. The shape is now displayed on the plane in the viewport [see Figure E2]. On the **Closed Shapes** section, turn on the **Render Outline** switch. On the **Outlines** section, set **Width** to **5**.

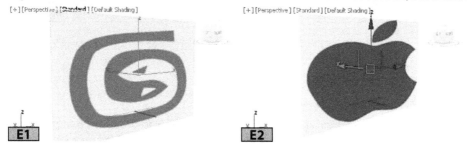

E1   E2

Set **Fill Color**, **Line Color**, **Background Color** to **RGB [141, 141, 141]**, **RGB [252, 255, 0]**, and **RGB [156, 188, 247]**, respectively. On the **Map Boundary** section, select **Manual** and then set **Width** and **Height** to **537**, and **300**, respectively. The logo is now centered on the plane [see Figure E3]. Take a render [see Figure E4]. Now, if zoom in on an area of the logo and then render, you would notice that you will still get a high resolution output [see Figure E5].

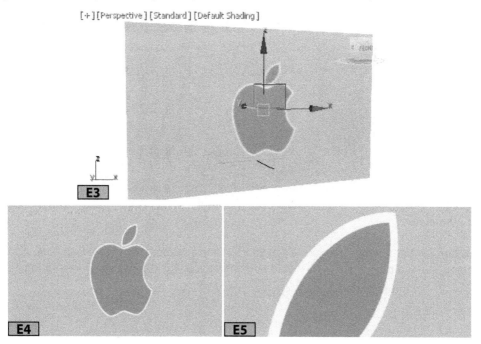

E3

E4   E5

Exercise 13: Working with Text Map

In this exercise, we will create a resolution independent map using the **Text Map**.

The following Table summarizes the exercise.

Table E13: Working with Text Map	
Topics in this section:	• Getting Ready • Working with Text Map
Skill Level	Beginner
Project Folder	**unit-mt3**
Start File	**umt3-hoe13-start.max**
Final Exercise File	**umt3-hoe19-end.max**
Time to Complete	20 Minutes

Getting Ready

Open **umt3-hoe13-start.max** in 3ds Max.

Working with the Text Map

Press **M** to open **Slate Material Editor** and then from the **Material/Map Browser | General | Maps** rollout, drag **Standard** to the active view. Connect **Text Map** to the **Diffuse** slot of the material. Select the plane in the viewport. RMB click on the material node and then choose **Assign Material to Selection**. Again, RMB click and then choose **Show Shaded Material in Viewport**. Notice only standard logo is displayed in the viewport at this moment [see Figure E1].

On the **Parameter Editor | Text Map | Text Parameters** rollout, click **None** and then click the **TextPlus** object in any viewport. The text is now displayed on the plane in the viewport [see Figure E2]. On the **Characters** section, turn on the **Render Outline** switch. On the **Outlines** section, set **Width** to **5**.

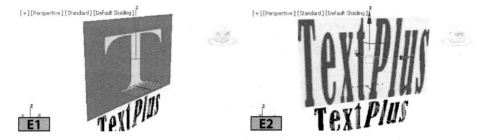

Set **Fill Color, Line Color, Background Color** to **RGB [141, 141, 141]**, **RGB [252, 255, 0]**, and **RGB [156, 188, 247]**, respectively. On the **Map Boundary** section, select **Manual** and then set **Width** and **Height** to **500**, and **200**, respectively.

The text is now centered on the plane [see Figure E3]. Take a render [see Figure E4]. Now, if zoom in on an area of the text and then render, you would notice that you will still get a high resolution output [see Figure E5].

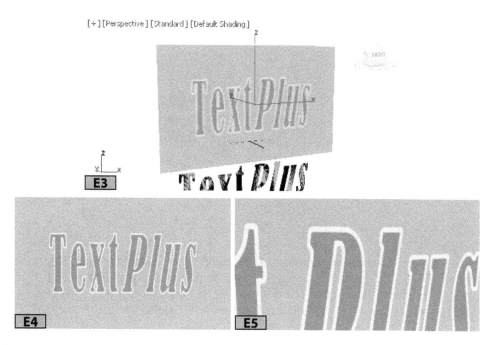

E3

E4

E5

Exercise 14: Working with TextureObjMask Map

In this exercise, we will create a resolution independent map using the **TextureObjMask** map.

The following Table summarizes the exercise.

Table E14: Working with TextureObjMask map	
Topics in this section:	• Getting Ready • Working with TextureObjMask Map
Skill Level	Beginner
Project Folder	**unit-mt3**
Start File	**umt3-hoe14-start.max**
Final Exercise File	**umt3-hoe14-end.max**
Time to Complete	20 Minutes

Getting Ready
Open **umt3-hoe20-start.max** in 3ds Max.

Working with the TextureObjMask Map
Press **M** to open **Slate Material Editor** and then drag **TextureObjMask** to the active view. On the **Parameter Editor | TextureObjMask | Parameters** rollout, click **Control Object's None** button and then click on the sphere in a viewport to make it the control object.

Now, drag the **Cellular** and **Noise** maps to the active view. Change the color as desired and then connect the **Cellular** map to the **Texture1** [outside texture] port of the **TextureObjMask** and the **Noise** map to the

Texture2 [inside texture] port [see Figure E1]. In the **Parameter Editor | TextureObjMask | Parameters** rollout, set **Transition Range** to **25**.

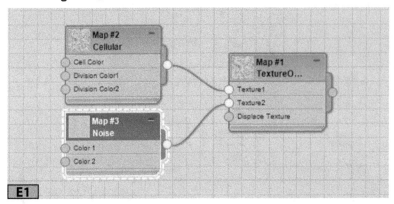

E1

Now, create a **Standard** material and connect its **Diffuse** port to the **TextureObjMask.** Select the plane in a viewport and RMB click on the material node and then choose **Assign Material to Selection**. Again, RMB click and then choose **Show Shaded Material in Viewport**. Take a test render [see Figure E2]. The sphere is obscuring the plane rendering. Create another **Standard** material and set its **Opacity** to **35**. Take a test render [see Figure E3].

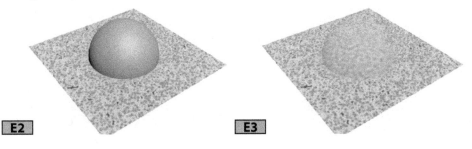

E2   E3

Quiz
Evaluate your skills to see how many questions you can answer correctly.

Multiple Choice
Answer the following questions, only one choice is correct.

1. Which of the following shading models is used to create realistic highlights for shiny, and regular surfaces?

   [A] **Phong**   [B] **Blinn**
   [C] **Metal**   [D] **Strauss**

2. Which of the following shading models is used to create surfaces with elliptical, anisotropic highlights?

   [A] **Phong**   [B] **Blinn**
   [C] **Metal**   [D] **Oren-Nayar-Blinn**

Fill in the Blanks

Fill in the blanks in each of the following statements:

1. The option in the _____ rollout are used by the **Architectural, Raytrace, Standard,** and **Ink 'n Paint** materials to improve the quality of the rendered image.

2. You can use the _____ shader to create realistic-looking metallic surfaces and a variety of organic-looking materials.

3. The _____ shader is a variant of the **Blinn** shader and can be used to model matte surfaces such as fabric.

4. The _____ material allows you to mix two materials on a single side of the surface.

5. The _____ material is used with the **Morpher** modifier.

6. The _____ material allows you to assign materials at the sub-object level.

7. The _____ material lets you assign two different materials to the top and bottom portions of an object.

8. The _____ material is used to make whole objects or any set of faces into matte objects.

9. The _____ material is used to create cartoons effects. This material produces shading with inked borders.

10. The _____ utility removes mapping coordinates or materials from the currently selected objects.

True or False

State whether each of the following is true or false:

1. Self-illuminated materials do not show shadows cast onto them. Also, they are unaffected by the lights in the scene.

2. The **Roughness** parameter is available only with the **Oren-Nayar-Blinn** and **Multi-Level** shaders, and with the **Physical** material.

3. The **Multi-Layer Shader** has three layers of specular highlights.

4. You can not use the **Quicksilver** hardware renderer to render **DirectX Shader** materials.

5. This **XRef** material lets you use a material applied to an object in another 3ds Max scene file.

Summary
The unit covered the following topics:

- General/Scanline materials
- General maps

Unit MT4–Physical and Autodesk Materials

The Autodesk materials are only visible in the **Material/Map Browser** if the active renderer is **ART** or **Quicksilver Hardware** renderer. The **Physical** material is physically-based material and it is compatible with both the **ART** and **Arnold** renderers. Autodesk Materials are used to model commonly used surfaces in the construction, design, and the environment. These materials correspond to the materials found in other Autodesk products such as **Autodesk AutoCAD**, **Revit** and **Autodesk Inventor**. So, if you work between these applications, you can share surface and material information among them.

In this unit, I'll describe the following:

- Autodesk Materials
- Physical Material

Autodesk Materials

Autodesk Materials work best when you use them with physically accurate lights such as photometric lights in a scene, modeled in the real-world units. Many of the Autodesk materials use **Autodesk Bitmaps**. The **Autodesk Bitmap** is a simple bitmap type. This bitmap type always uses the real-world mapping coordinates. Therefore, if you have applied a **UVW Map** modifier to any geometry, make sure you turn on **Real-World Map Size** on the **Parameters** rollout. You can also change the default bitmap assignment.

Caution: Autodesk Bitmap compatibility
*3ds Max allows you to disconnect a bitmap, or replace it with another map. However, if you disconnect an **Autodesk Bitmap** in other application such as **Autodesk AutoCAD**, you won't be able to read the Autodesk material. If you are using other applications, make sure that you do not replace the bitmap with a map that only 3ds Max understands.*

Warning: Autodesk Material Library
*If you uninstall or remove Autodesk material library, the materials will no longer will be available for other Autodesk products such as **AutoCAD**, **Revit**, or **Inventor**.*

Autodesk Ceramic
You can use this material to model the glazed ceramic material including porcelain.

Open **autoMat_begin.max**. Open **Slate Material Editor**. On **Material/Map Browser | Materials | Autodesk**, double-click on **Autodesk Ceramic** to display the material's interface in the active view [see Figure F1]. Double-click on the material's node in the active view. In the **Property Editor | Ceramic** rollout, ensure that **Ceramic** is selected as **Type**. The **Ceramic** type produces look of earthenware.

Apply the material to teapot in the scene and render the scene[see Figure F2]. On the **Ceramic** rollout, set **Type** to **Porcelain**. Click **Color** swatch and change color to blue.

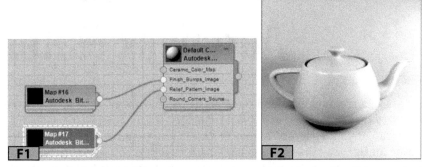

Color sets the color of the material. The other two options available for the **Color** control are **Use Map** and **Color By Object**. The **Use Map** option allows you to assign a map to color component of the material. If you set **Color** to **Color By Object**, 3ds Max uses the object's wireframe color as the material color. The **Finish** control lets you adjust the finish and reflectivity of the material.

Note: Color by object
*When you use the **Color By Object** option, the color appears on rendering but not in the viewport or material previews.*

Make sure **Finish** is set to **High Gloss / Glazed** and render the scene[see Figure 3]. Make sure **Finish** is set to **Satin** and render the scene[see Figure F4]. Make sure **Finish** is set to **Matte** and render the scene [see Figure F5]. Now, set **Finish** to **High Gloss / Glazed**.

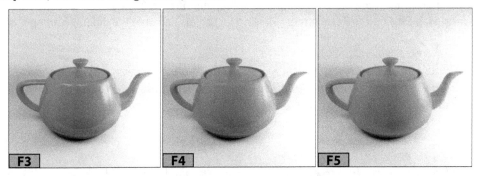

On the **Finish Bumps** rollout, check **Enable** and make sure **Type** is set to **Wavy** and **Amount** to **0.3**. Now, render the scene [see Figure F6].

The options in the **Finish Bumps** rollout can be used to simulate the patterns that appear in glaze during firing. You can also create custom bumps by using the **Custom** option from the **Type** drop-down. **Amount** sets the strength of the pattern to apply.

On the **Finish Bumps** rollout, turn off **Enable**. On the **Relief Pattern** rollout, turn on **Enable**. Click the **Image** button. On the **Parameters** rollout, click **Source None** button. Select **pattern.jpg** from the **Select**

Bitmap Image File dialog and click **Open**. On the **Relief Pattern** rollout, set **Amount** to **1.2** and render the scene[see Figure F7].

The options in the **Relief Pattern** rollout allow you to model a pattern stamped into the clay. **Amount** controls the height of the relief pattern.

Autodesk Concrete

This material allows you to model the concrete material. Figure F8 shows its interface. The **Sealant** control of the **Concrete** rollout, controls the reflectiveness of the surface. **None** [see Figure F9] does not affect the surface finish. **Epoxy** [see Figure F10] adds a reflective coating on the surface whereas **Acrylic** [see Figure F11] adds a matte reflective coating.

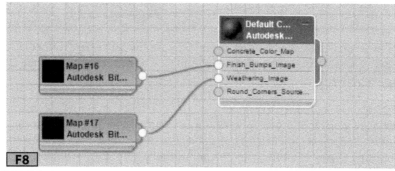

The **Type** control in the **Finish Bumps** area allows you to set the texture of the concrete. **Broom Straight** which is a default type, specifies a straight broom pattern [see Figure F12]. **Broom Curved** uses a curving broom pattern [see Figure F13]. **Smooth** creates a pattern with speckled irregularities [see Figure F14].

Polished uses a completely smooth pattern [see Figure F15]. **Stamped/Custom** allows you to specify a bitmap for generating the pattern [see Figure F16].

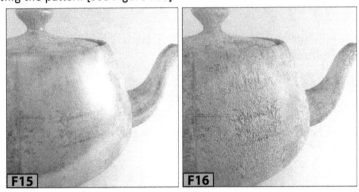

Weathering applies a slight variation in the brightness on the surface of the concrete. The default weathering method is **Automatic** that applies weathering automatically. You can use **Custom** to specify a custom weathering pattern.

Autodesk Generic

This material provides a generic interface for creating a custom appearance. You can convert an Autodesk material to the **Autodesk Generic** material by RMB clicking on the node in the **Slate Material Editor | Active View** and then choosing **Copy as Generic** from the popup menu.

Autodesk Glazing

This material allows you to model a thin and transparent material such as glazing in windows and doors. The **Color** control in the **Glazing** rollout lets you choose the color for the sheet of glass. Figure F17 shows the teapot rendered with the **Blue Green** color applied to it.

Autodesk Harwood

This material is used the model the appearance of a wood. The **Stain** control in the **Wood** rollout allows you to choose a stain to add to the base harwood pattern. Figure F18 shows the wood material with **Brown Stain** color.

The **Finish** control lets you choose the surface finish of the harwood. The **Glossy Varnish** is the default option [see Figure F18]. The other options available are: **Semi-Gloss Varnish** [see Figure F19], **Satin Varnish** [see Figure F20], and **Unfinished** [see Figure F21].

The **Used For** control lets you adjust the appearance of the wood. **Flooring** uses an ocean shader that adds a slight warp to the large surfaces, improving the realism. When you choose **Furniture**, the surfaces are not warped. However, you can use the **Relief Pattern** map to achieve various effects.

When you check **Enable** in the **Relief Pattern** rollout, **mental ray** generates a relief pattern like bump map on the wood surface. The **Type** control lets you choose the relief pattern. When you choose **Based on wood grain**, it generates a relief pattern based on the image map used to create the wood pattern. **Custom** allows you to choose a custom map for the relief pattern. **Amount** lets you adjust the height of the relief pattern.

Autodesk Masonry/CMU

This material can be used to model masonry or concrete masonry units [**CMUs**]. Figure F22 and F23 shows the brick and CMU material.

Autodesk Metal

You can use this material to model various metallic surfaces. The **Type** control in the **Metal** rollout lets you choose the type of material you want to create. These materials define the base color and texture of the material. Figure F24 show the brass material. The **Finish** control lets you choose the surface finish for the surface. Figures F24 and F25 show the brass material with the **Polished** and **Brushed** finish, respectively.

Autodesk Metallic Paint

This material allows you to model a metallic paint surface such as paint of a car [see Figure F26].

F24 F25 F26

Autodesk Mirror

This material lets you model a mirror material [see Figure F27].

Autodesk Plastic/Vinyl

This material allows you to model the surfaces that have a synthetic appearance such as plastic or vinyl [see Figures F28 and F29].

F27 F28 F29

Autodesk Point Cloud Material

This is a special purpose material that is automatically applied to any point-cloud object in the scene. This material allows you to control the overall color intensity, ambient occlusion, and shadows.

Autodesk Solid Glass

This material allows you to model the appearance of the solid glass [see Figure F30].

Autodesk Stone

You can use this material to create the appearance of the stone [see Figures F31 and F32]. The **Type** control in the **Finish Bumps** rollout lets you specify the bump pattern. Available options are: **Polished Granite**, **Stone Wall**, **Glossy Marble**, and **Custom**.

Autodesk Wall Paint

This material can be used to model the appearance of a painted surface such as paint on the walls of a room [see Figures F33 and F34]. The **Application** control in the **Wall Paint** rollout lets you choose the texture method. In other words, you can control how paint is applied on the surface. **Roller** is the default method. Other two methods are **Brush** and **Spray**.

Autodesk Water

This material can be used to model appearance of a water surface [see Figure F35]. The **Type** control in the **Water** rollout lets you choose the scale and texture of the water.

The available options are **Swimming Pool, Generic Reflective Pool, Generic Stream/River, Generic Pond/ Lake**, and **Generic Sea/Ocean**. The **Color** control lets you specify the color of the water. This option is only available for **Generic Stream/River, Pond/Lake**, and **Sea/Ocean**.

The following options are available for adjusting the color of the water: **Tropical, Algae/Green, Murky/ Brown, Generic Reflecting Pool, Generic Stream/River, Generic Pond/Lake, Generic Sea/Ocean** and **Custom**.

Physical Material

Physical material allows you to model shading effects of the real-world materials with ease. This material is the layered material that gives you ability to efficiently use the physically-based workflows. This material is compatible with **ART** and **Arnold** renderers. Do not use the legacy **Scanline** renderer with it as **Scanline** renderer shows just the approximation of the shader and does not support many crucial features.

This material is comprised of the following:

- A base layer that represents a diffuse color or colored metallic reflections. There can be an option clear-coat layer at the top. The clear-coat layer stays at the top of all layers and reduces energy based on how much energy it reflects and transparency color of the coating.

- Transparency layer
- Sub-surface scattering/translucency layer
- Emission [Self-Illumination] layer. This layer does not participate in the energy conversation and adds energy.

According to the energy conservation model of this material, the sum of various shading components can not exceed 100%. One exception is emission, in this case, energy is added. The energy calculation is based on the weight parameters instead of color parameters. This material ensures that the light does not amplify. When the **Metalness** parameter of the material is set to **1**, the material is opaque. It does not produce any Diffuse, Transparency, or Sub-surface Scattering effects.

Physical Material comes with number of presets that you can use as a quick starting point. You can select the presets from the **Presets** rollout of the material. The **Material mode** drop-down also in the **Presets** rollout, lets you choose a mode. The two available modes are **Standard** and **Advanced**. The **Advanced** mode is the superset of the **Standard** mode with hidden parameters. In most of the cases, the parameters in the **Standard** mode are sufficient to make physically plausible materials. Some of the advanced parameters are: **Reflection Color** and **Weight**, **Diffuse Roughness**, and controls in the **Advanced Reflectance Parameters** rollout.

Hands-on Exercises

From the **File** menu, choose **Set Project Folder** to open the **Browse for Folder** dialog. Navigate to the folder where you want to save the files and then click **Make New Folder**. Create the new folder with the name **unit-mt4** and click **OK** to create the project directory.

Exercise 1: Creating Glossy Varnished Wood

In this exercise, we're going to create a varnished glossy wood material using **Physical Material** [see Figure E1].

The following table summarizes the exercise.

Table E9: Creating Glossy Varnished Wood	
Topics in this section:	• Getting Ready • Creating the Material
Skill Level	Intermediate
Project Folder	**unit-mt4**
Start File	**umt4-physical-mat-start.max**
Final Exercise File	**umt4-hoe1-end.max, umt4-hoe1-end-2.max**
Time to Complete	20 Minutes

Getting Ready

Open the **umt4-physical-mat-start.max**.

Creating the Material

Apply **Physical Material** to the **geo1**, **geo2**, and **geo3** geometries in the scene. Rename the material as **glossyVarnishedMat**. On the **Parameter Editor | Presets** rollout, select **Standard** from the **Material mode** drop-down, if not already selected. On the **Parameter Editor | glossyVarnishedMat | Basic Parameters** rollout | **Base Color and Reflections** section, click **Base Color's** button. On the **Material/Map Browser | Maps | General** rollout, double-click **Bitmap**. On the **Select Bitmap Image File** dialog, choose **wooden-plank-1. jpeg**. Also, set gamma override to **2.2**.

The first spinner in the **Base Color** section is **Weight**, the relative measurement of the base color. The value in this spinner participate in the energy conversion. You can use the button next to **Weight** to assign a map to it. The Color swatch next to the **Weight** spinner is the base color of the material. For non-metals, this swatch defines the diffuse color. For metals, it defines the color of the metal itself. Render the scene[see Figure E2].

Notice the render in Figure E2, the wood is highly reflective, we need to add some roughness to the reflection and transparency components.

On the **Reflections** section, set **Roughness** to **0.9** and then render the scene[see Figure E3]. Notice that setting **Roughness** to **0.9**, the material has lost its gloss and looks very flat. Glossiness is the effectively the inverse of the roughness. If you enable the **Inv** switch corresponding to the **Roughness** parameter, it will yield glossy material. The **Roughness** parameter lets you control the roughness of the material. A higher **Roughness** value yields a blurrier result. You can lower the **Roughness** value to make the mirror like material.

Enable the **Inv** switch and then set **IOR** to **1.7**.

The **IOR** parameter controls the index of refraction level of the material. If defines how much rays bend when they enter a medium. It also affects the angular dependency of the reflectivity when set to the default **Fresnel** mode [see the **Advanced Reflectance Parameters** rollout]. On the **Transparency** section, click the **Lock** icon and then set **Roughness** to **1**. Also, enable the **Inv** switch. Render the scene[see Figure E4].

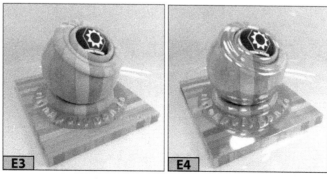

By default, roughness values of reflectivity and transparency are locked together. You can unlink them clicking the **Lock** icon.

E5

On the **Anisotropy** rollout, select **Map channel** and then set **Channel** to **1**. Set **Anisotropy** and **Rotation** to **0.4**, and **0.3**, respectively. Render the scene [see Figure E5].

The **Anisotropy** parameter controls the U-direction roughness in relation to the V-direction roughness. The **Rotation** parameter controls the anisotropy angle. This control ranges from **0** to **1** which represents one full revolution. The **Auto** option automatically orients the anisotropy whereas the **Map channel** option orients the anisotropy based on a given texture space.

Now, we will create a bump map using the **Noise** map.

Drag a **Noise** map to the active view. On the **Parameter Editor | Noise** map | **Coordinates** rollout, set **Source** to **Explicit Map Channel** and ensure **Map Channel** is set to **1**. Set **Tiling U, V,** and **W** to **0.5, 200,** and **100,** respectively. On the **Noise Parameters** rollout, set **Size** to **0.2** [see Figure E6]. Set **Color #1** to **RGB[180, 180, 180]**. Drag a **Mix** map to the active view. Connect **Noise** map to the **Color 1** port of the **Mix** map and **Bitmap** to the **Color 2** port. Connect the **Mix** map to the **Bump Map** port of **glossyVarnishedMat** [see Figure E7]. On the **Parameter Editor | Mix** map | **Mix Parameters** rollout, set **Mix Amount** to **30**.

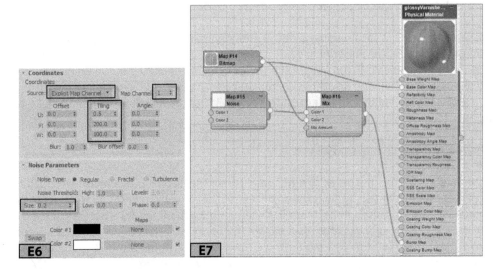

E6

E7

Take the final render [see Figure E1]. Now, if you want to create a less glossy satin varnished wood material, you need to lower down the reflection **Roughness** and **IOR** values [see Figure E8].

Check the **umt4-hoe1-end-2.max** file for the satin varnished material.

Exercise 2: Creating Glass Materials

In this exercise, we're going to create a glass materials using the **Physical** material.

The following table summarizes the exercise.

Table E2: Creating the Glass Materials	
Topics in this section:	• Getting Ready • Creating the Materials
Skill Level	Intermediate
Project Folder	**unit-mt4**
Start File	**umt4-physical-mat-start.max**
Final Exercise File	**umt4-hoe2-end.max**
Time to Complete	20 Minutes

Getting Ready
Open the **umt4-physical-mat-start.max** file.

Creating the Materials
Apply **Physical Material** to **Geo1**, **Geo2**, and **Geo3** in the scene. Rename the material as **glassMat**. On the **Parameter Editor | glassMat** material | **Presets** rollout, choose **Advanced** from the **Material mode** drop-down.

There are two types of modes available for the **Physical** material: **Standard** and **Advanced**. When you choose the **Standard** mode, you get access to the parameters that you can use to create most physically plausible materials. The **Advanced** mode gives you access to advanced reflection, roughness, and weight parameters. You can use these parameters to create advanced materials.

On the **glassMat** material | **Basic Parameters** rollout | **Base Color** section, set **Base Color** weight to **0**. The material turns black. On the **Transparency** section, set the **Transparency** weight to **1** to make the glass completely transparent. Render the scene [see Figure E1]. On the **Reflections** section, set **IOR** to **1.7**.

The **IOR** value sets the **Index of Refraction** level. It controls how much rays bend when entering in a medium.

Turn on the **Thin-walled** switch and render the scene [see Figure E2].

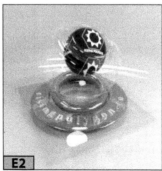

When this switch is turned on, the object is considered to be made out of an infinitely thin transparent shell. This shell us not reflective. Also, the transparency depth is disabled and the sub-surface scattering is replaced by translucency.

Turn off the **Thin-walled** switch.

You can create tinted glass by specifying a color for **Transparency** and specifying a depth. In the **Transparency** section, set color to **Red** and then set **Depth** to **0.05** and render the scene [see Figure E3].

You can create some interesting effects by using sub-surface scattering option. On the **Sub-Surface Scattering** section, set color to yellow and take a test render. Notice that there is no change in the color of the glass. As discussed earlier, the sum of various shading components can not exceed 100%, therefore, you need to reduce weight of other parameter to see the effect of sub-surface scattering.

On the **Transparency** section, set **weight** to **0.85** and render the scene [see Figure E4].

Exercise 3: Creating Metal Materials

In this exercise, we're going to create a metal materials using **Physical Material**.

The following table summarizes the exercise.

Table E3: Creating the Metal Materials	
Topics in this section:	• Getting Ready • Creating the Materials
Skill Level	Intermediate
Project Folder	**unit-mt4**
Start File	**umt4-physical-mat-start.max**
Final Exercise File	**umt4-hoe3-end.max**
Time to Complete	20 Minutes

Getting Ready

Open the **umt4-physical-mat-start.max** file.

Creating the Materials

Apply **Physical Material** to **Geo1**, **Geo2**, and **Geo3** in the scene. Rename the material as **metalMat**. On the **Parameter Editor | metalMat** material | **Presets** rollout, choose **Advanced** from the **Material mode** drop-down.

First, we will create highly reflective material. On the **metalMat** material | **Basic Parameters** rollout | **Base Color** section, set **Base Color** weight to **0**. On the **Reflections** section, set **IOR** to **48** and then render the scene [see Figure E1]. The reflection in the material is coming from the gray background. If you want more reflections in the metal, use a reflection map.

Now, if you want to create a material like aluminium, blur the reflections by adding some roughness to the metal. On the **Reflections** section, set **Roughness** to **0.3** and then render the scene [see Figure E2]. You can make the metal darker by darkening the **Reflection** color. Set it to medium gray and render the scene [see Figure E3].

If you want to add of the weight of the base color to the material, it will have no effect because of the high **IOR** value. If you use low **IOR** value, you loose the metal look. To compensate for this, you can use the **Metalness** parameter. If you set **Metalness** to **1**, you do not see the base layer, just the colored reflections.

On the **Parameter Editor | metalMat | Basic Parameters** rollout | **Base Color** section, set base color to **RGB [0.82, 0.416, and 0.099]** and weight to **0.3**. On the **Reflections** section, set reflection color to **RGB [0.584, 0.584, 0.584]**, weight to **0.7**, **Roughness** to **0.3**, **Metalness** to **0.5**, and **IOR** to **6**. Render the scene [see Figure E4].

Quiz
Evaluate your skills to see how many questions you can answer correctly.

Multiple Choice
Answer the following questions, only one choice is correct.

1. Which of the following renderers support **Autodesk** Materials?

   [A] **Quicksilver Hardware**   [B] **ART**
   [C] A and B   [D] None of these

2. Which of the following options are available in the **Material** mode drop-down of **Physical Material**?

   [A] **Standard**   [B] **Advanced**
   [C] A and B   [D] None of these

Fill in the Blanks
Fill in the blanks in each of the following statements:

1. **Physical Material** is physically-based material and it is compatible with both the _____ and _____ renderers.

2. According to the energy conservation model of **Physical Material**, the sum of various shading components can not exceed _____ %.

3. The _____ parameter controls relative measurement of the color of the corresponding component.

4. The _____ parameter controls the index of refraction level of the material.

5. The _____ parameter controls the U-direction roughness in relation to the V-direction roughness.

True or False
State whether each of the following is true or false:

1. **Autodesk Bitmap** always uses the real-world mapping coordinates.

2. The **Scanline** renderer shows just the approximation of **Physical Material** and does not support many crucial features.

3. When the **Metalness** parameter of **Physical Material** is set to **1**, the material becomes transparent.

Summary
The unit covered the following topics:

- Autodesk Materials
- Physical Material

MT4-14   Unit MT4 - Physical and Autodesk Materials

Unit ML1: Standard Lighting

To achieve professional-quality, realistic renders in 3ds Max, you need to master the art of lighting. Lights play an important role in the visual process. They shape the world we see. The trick to simulate realistic looking light effects is to observe the world around us. The lights you create in a scene, illuminate other objects in the scene. The material applied to the objects simulates color and texture.

In this unit, I will describe the following:

- Basic Lighting Concepts
- Creating and placing lights
- 3ds Max Lights
- Light Linking
- Shadows
- Lighting Effects

The reasons to add the light objects to the scene are as follows:

- They improve the illumination of the scene.
- They enhance the realism of the scene through realistic lighting effects.
- They give depth to the scene by casting shadows.
- They enhance the scene by projecting maps onto the scene.
- They also help in modeling light source such as headlights of a car.
- They create lights using files from manufactures [such as IES files].

Note: IES Lights
You can use these lights to visualize the commercially available lighting in your scene by adding **Photometric** *lights to the scene.*

Standard Lights

The standard lights in 3ds Max are computer based lights that simulate lights such as lamps and bulbs. Unlike **Photometric** lights, these lights do not have the physically-based intensity values. To create a light, on the **Create** panel, click **Lights**. Choose **Standard** from the drop-down available below **Lights** and then on the **Object Type** rollout, click the type of light you want to create. Now, click on a viewport to create the light. The creation method in the viewport depends on the type of light you have chosen. For example, if a light has target, you need to click-drag to set the target.

Whenever you create a light in the scene, the default lighting is turned off. It will be restored when you delete all lights from the scene. Like all objects in 3ds Max, lights have name, and color. You can set these options from the **Name and Color** rollout.

Note: The color of the light
The color that you set for the light from the **Name and Color** *rollout only changes the color of the light geometry in the scene. It has no effect on the color cast by the light.*

Note: Default Lighting

When there are no light objects in the scene, 3ds Max illuminates the scene using the default lighting. The default lighting disappears as soon as you add a light object to the scene. When you delete all light objects from the scene, the default lighting reappears.

Now, let's explore the standard lights.

Target Spotlight

The target spotlight casts a focused beam of light. You can use this light to simulate flashlight, a follow spot on a stage, or the headlights of the car. To create a target spotlight, click **Target Spot** from the **Object Type** rollout. Now, drag in a viewport to place the light. The initial point of the drag defines the location of the spotlight whereas the point at which you release the mouse defines the location of the target. In Figure F1, I have marked light with 1 and its target with 2.

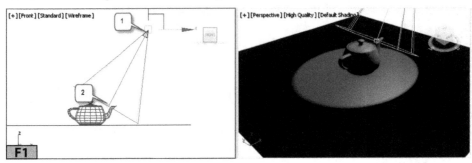

Note: Light and its target

*When you create a light that has a target, two objects will appear in **Scene Explorer**: light object and its target. The target name has an extension **.target**. For example, if you create a spot light in the scene, the name of the light and its target will be as follows: **Spot001** and **Spot001.Target**. When you rename a light, its target object will be automatically renamed accordingly. However, remember that renaming a target object does not rename its parent light.*

Note: Free Spotlight

Free Spotlight *is similar to **Target Spotlight** except the difference that it has no target. You can move and rotate **Free Spotlight** to aim in any direction.*

To adjust the target, select it in a viewport or from **Scene Explorer** and then move the target using the **Select and Move** tool. The spotlight is always aimed at its target. The distance of the target from the light does not affect the attenuation or brightness of the light.

You can also change a viewport to a light view so that the viewport shows the light's point of view. This feature is immensely helpful in placing the lights correctly. To change a viewport to a light view, click or RMB click on **POV** label. Now, choose **Lights | Name** of the light from the menu. Figure F2 shows the point of view of the light that was shown in Figure F1.

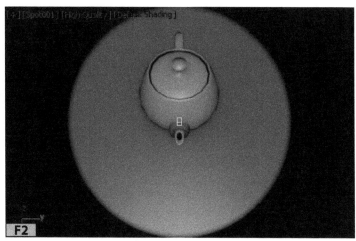

You can change the properties of the spot light from the rollouts available in the **Modify** panel. Let's explore the controls available in these rollouts.

General Parameters Rollout

This rollout is displayed for the **Standard** lights. The controls in this rollout allow you to turn light on or off, exclude or include objects in the scene, and change the type of light. You can also toggle the shadow casting from this rollout.

To turn a light on or off, toggle the **On** switch from this rollout. The drop-down on the right of the **On** switch lets you switch between the light types. When the **Targeted** switch is on, the light is targeted. When on, the distance between the light and its target is displayed on the right of this switch.

To toggle shadow casting, use the **On** switch from the **Shadows** section. Turn on the **Use Global Settings** switch to use the global settings for shadows that are cast by this light. The shadow parameters defined by the light are shared with all the lights of same class. When off, the shadow parameters are specific to that light.

The drop-down in the **Shadows** group lets you choose the algorithm to be used by the light to cast shadows. The following table summarizes various algorithms.

Table 1: The shadow generating algorithms	
Algorithm	**Description**
Shadow Map	The shadow map is a bitmap that is generated during a pre-rendering pass of the scene. This map doesn't show the color cast by transparent or translucent objects. A shadow map can produce soft-edged shadows that cannot be generated by a ray-traced shadow [see Figure F3]. Also, depth map shadows take less time to render than the ray-traced shadows. You can change the shadow map options from the **Shadows Map Parameters** rollout.

Table 1: The shadow generating algorithms	
Algorithm	**Description**
Ray-Traced Shadows/Adv. Ray-Traced Shadows	The **Ray-traced shadows** [see Figure F4] are more accurate than the shadow-mapped shadows and are generated by tracing the path of the rays sampled from a light source. They create better results for the transparent or translucent objects. Only ray-traced shadows can generate shadows for the wireframed objects. The **Adv. Ray-Traced Shadows** are same as ray-traced shadows, however they provide anti-aliasing controls to fine tune the shadows.
Area Shadows	This algorithm simulates shadows generated by a light with area of volume. You can change volume type from the drop-down available in the **Basic Options** group of the **Area Shadows** rollout. Figure F5 shows the shadows generated by using the **Box Light** volume.

Tip: Transparent and Translucent objects

If you want convincing looking shadow results for the transparent and translucent objects, use raytraced or advance raytraced shadows.

Tip: Preventing an object from casting shadows

*You can prevent an object from casting shadows in the scene, to do this, select the object and then RMB click. Choose **Object Properties** from the **Quad** menu and then turn off the **Cast Shadows** switch from the **Rendering Control** group of the **Object Properties** dialog.*

You can also exclude the selected object from the effects of the lights. This feature is very useful when you want a light to lit specific objects in the scene. Click **Exclude** to open the **Exclude/Include** dialog [see Figure F6].

Now, select the objects that you want to affect from the **Scene Objects** section of the dialog. Select **Include** or **Exclude** from the right of the dialog. Now, click **>>** to add the selected object to the right pane of the dialog. You can click **<<** to move objects from right pane to the left pane. You have three options to control the effect: **Illumination**, **Shadow Casting**, and **Both**. You can use these options to exclude/include illumination, shadows, or both. Now, click **OK** to close the dialog and include/exclude objects with the light.

Intensity/Color/Attenuation Rollout

The controls in this rollout let you set the color and intensity of the light. Also, you can define the attenuation of the light. The **Multiplier** control amplifies the power of the light. You can use negative values to reduce the illumination. High **Multiplier** values wash out the colors whereas the negative values darkens the objects. The color swatch next to the **Multiplier** controls lets you select a color to be cast by the light.

Tip: Flashing light on and off
*Animate the **Multiplier** value to **0** [0 and 1] in repeated keyframes and then assign step tangent to the **Multiplier's** graph.*

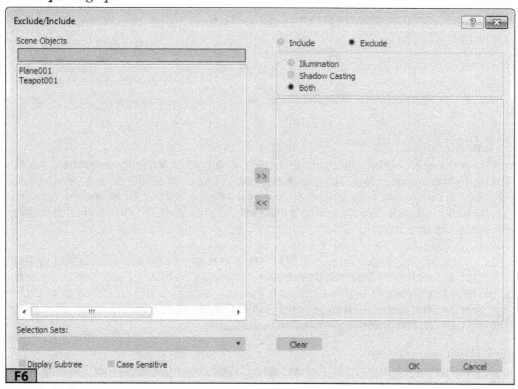

F6

The controls in the **Decay** group lets you control the light's intensity over distance. The following table summarizes the options available in the **Type** drop-down.

Table 2: The decay types	
Type	**Description**
None	No decay is applied [see the left image in Figure F7]. The light retains its full strength.
Inverse	It applies inverse decay [see the middle image in Figure F7]. The formula used to calculate decay is **luminance=RO/R**. **RO** is the radial source of the light of no attenuation is used. **R** is the radial distance of the illuminated surface from **RO**.
Inverse Square	It applies inverse-square decay [see the right image in Figure F7]. The formula used is **(RO/R)2**. This decay type is used by the **Photometric** lights and it is the real-world decay of the light.

F7

If you don't use the attenuation settings [discussed next], the **Start** control sets the distance at which the light begins to decay. You can use the **Show** switch to display the decay range in the viewports. For spotlights, the decay range appears as lens-shaped section of the cone [see the left image in Figure F8]. For directional light, it appears as circular section of the cone [see the middle image in Figure F8]. For omni lights and spot or directional lights with **Overshoot** turned on, the range appears as a sphere [see the right image in Figure F8].

F8

Attenuation is the effect of the light diminishing over distance. **Far Attenuation** controls the distance at which the light drops off to zero. The **Near Attenuation** value controls the distance at which the light fades in. You can turn on the attenuation from the **Near Attenuation** and **Far Attenuation** groups of the **Intensity/Color/Attenuation** rollout by using the **Use** control. The **Start** and **End** controls in these groups define the attenuation distances.

When you set the **Far Attenuation** value, the light intensity remains at the value specified by **Multiplier** up to the distance specified by **Start** and then drops off to zero at the distance specified by the **End**. When you set the **Near Attenuation** value, the light intensity remains zero up to the distance specified by **Start** and then from the **Start** to the distance specified by the **End**, the light intensity increases. Beyond **End**, the light intensity remains at the value specified by **Multiplier**.

Spotlight Parameters Rollout

The parameters in this rollout controls the hotspot and falloff properties of the spotlight. The **Show Cone** switch displays the cone in the viewport. The cone is always visible when a light is selected. This switch allows you to show the cone even if the light is not selected. When the **Overshoot** switch is on, the light casts light in all directions [not just within the cone] but the shadows and projections appear within the cone. The **Hotspot/Beam** and **Falloff/Field** parameters control the angle of the light's cone and light's falloff, respectively.

The **Circle** and **Rectangle** parameters define the shape of the falloff and hotspot areas. The **Aspect** parameter controls the aspect ratio of the rectangular light beam. The **Bitmap Fit** button lets you specify the aspect ratio as per the supplied bitmap.

Advanced Effects Rollout

The parameters in this rollout define how light affects the surfaces. Also, you can create projector lights. The **Contrast** parameter adjusts the ambient and diffuse areas of the surface. The default value is zero for this parameter that creates normal contrast. The **Soften Diff Edge** parameter, softens the edge between the diffuse and ambient components. The **Diffuse** switch when on, affects the **Diffuse** properties of an object's surface. Similarly, the **Specular** and **Ambient Only** switches can be used to affect the specular and ambient components, respectively.

The parameters in the **Projector Map** group let you make a light a projector. To create a projector light, open **Material Editor** and then create a map. Drag the map from **Material Editor** to the **None** button in the **Projector Map** section. Select **Instance** from the dialog that appears and click **OK**. The name of the map appears as button's label. Notice in Figure F9, I have used a **Cellular** map to project it on the teapot using a spotlight.

Atmospheres and Effects Rollout

You can use this rollout to assign, delete, and edit parameters for various atmospheric and rendering effects associated with the light. For example, to create the volume fog effect, click **Add** to open the **Add Atmosphere or Effect** dialog. Select **Volume Light** from the list and then click **OK** to close the dialog. In the **Atmospheres and Effects** rollout, select **Volume Light** and then click **Setup** to open the **Environments and Effects** dialog. Now, you can adjust the parameters from the **Atmosphere** rollout. Render the scene to see the effect. Notice in Figure F10, I have projected the **Cellular** map and then added volume effect to it.

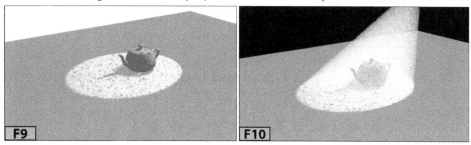

Shadow Parameters Rollout

The parameters in this rollout are displayed for all light types expect **Skylight**. You can use these parameters to define the shadow color and other general shadow properties. Use the **Color** swatch to change the color of the shadows. You can also animate the shadow color. **Dens** controls the density [darkness] of the shadows. You can also assign negative values to **Dens** that allows you to simulate the reflected light. Turn on the **Map** switch to assign a map to the shadows using the button available on its right. The process to add the map is the same as discussed with the projector light. Figure F11 shows the **Dent** map applied to the shadows. When the **Light Affects Shadow Color** switch is on, the color of the light blends with the color of the shadow.

Turn on the **On** switch in the **Atmosphere Shadows** section to allows atmospheric shadows to cast shadows as light passes through them. The **Opacity** parameter defines the opacity of the atmospheric shadows whereas the **Color Amount** parameter defines the amount of atmosphere color bleed into the shadows.

Shadow Map Params Rollout

This rollout is displayed when you choose the **Shadow Map** method for generating shadows. The **Bias** parameter moves the shadow toward or away from the shadow-casting objects. Figure F12 shows the render with **Bias** set to **1** and **3**, respectively. The **Size** parameter defines the size of the shadow map in square pixel computed for the light. Higher the value of Size, more detailed map will be. The **Sample Range** parameter controls how much area in the shadow is averaged. This settings effects the edges of the shadow. On increasing this value, blends the shadow edges and remove the granularity from the shadow.

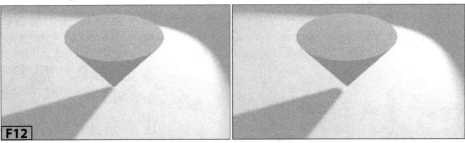

The **Absolute Map Bias** switch works with the **Bias** parameter. If you specify a low value for **Bias**, the shadows can leak and if you specify a too high value, the shadow might detach from the object. Setting an extremes value in either case might result in no shadows at all. This behavior depends on the **Absolute Map Bias** switch. When off, the **Bias** is calculated based on the scene extents and then it is normalized to one. This results in similar results regardless of the size of the scene. When on, the **Bias** value is treated in 3ds Max scene units and the result is dependent on the size of the scene.

When **2 Sided Shadow** switch is on, blackfaces are not ignored when calculating shadows. Figure F13 shows the render of the teapot with the **2 Sided Shadows** switch turned on and off, respectively.

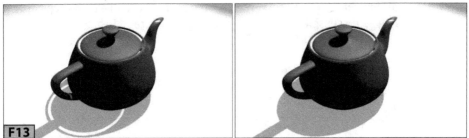

The type of renderer you choose will also affect your choice of shadow algorithm used. The **Quicksilver Hardware** renderer always casts shadow-mapped shadows. The following table summarizes the shadow types the **Scanline** and **mental ray** renderers support.

Table 3: The shadow types supported by the **Scanline** and **mental ray** renderers

Type	Scanline	mental ray
Advanced Ray-Traced	Yes	No
mental ray Shadow Map	No	Yes
Area	Yes	No
Shadow Map	Yes	Yes
Ray-Traced	Yes	Yes

The following table summarizes the pro and cons of each shadow type:

Table 4: Shadow types comparison		
Type	**Pros**	**Cons**
Advanced Ray-Traced	Supports opacity and transparency. It uses less memory than the raytraced shadows. This type is recommended for complex scenes with lots of light.	It is slower than the shadow map and computed at every frame. It does not support soft shadows.
Area	Supports opacity and transparency and uses very less RAM. It supports different format for area shadows.	It is slower than the shadow map and computed at every frame.
Shadow Map	Fastest shadow type. It produces soft shadows. It is computed once if there is no animated object present in the scene.	Uses a lot of RAM and does not support objects with transparency and opacity maps.
Ray-Traced	Supports transparency and opacity mapping. It is computed once if there is no animated object present in the scene.	It does not support soft shadows. It is slower than the shadows maps.

Ray Traced Shadow Params Rollout

This rollout is displayed when you choose the **Ray Traced Shadows** method for generating shadows. The **Ray Bias** control moves the shadow toward or away from the shadow casting object. The **Max Quadtree Depth** control sets the depth of Quadtree used by the raytracer. Higher the value you specify for this control, more enhanced the results will be. However, you will be taxed on the render time.

Note: Quadtree

Quadtree is the data structure used by the raytracer. It represents scene from the point of the view of the light. The root node of the Quadtree contains all visible objects in the scene. If there are too many objects available in the scene, four more nodes [leaf nodes] are generated to hold these objects. This process continue adaptively until each node has a small number of objects and Quadtree depth limit is achieved. The maximum size of a Quadtree is the square of two to the power of the maximum Quadtree depth. For example, at the depth of 7, the total number of the leaf node generated will be $2^7 * 2^7 = 128 * 128 = 16384$.

Warning: Omni Light and Quadtree

An omni light can generate up to ten Quadtrees, therefore, if you are using raytraced shadows, it will use more memory and render time.

Tip: The raytraced shadows and renderers

Both the Scanline renderer and mental ray renderer support raytraced shadows. If you are using the Scanline renderer, the Adv Ray Traced method gives you more control over the shadows.

Adv. Ray Traced Params Rollout

The parameters in this rollout allow you to control the advanced raytraced shadows. These shadows are similar to the raytraced shadows, however, they give you more control over the shadows. The drop-down in the **Basic Options** group allows you to select type of raytracing. The **Simple** type casts a single ray of light toward the surface. No antialiasing is performed when you select this type.

Shadow Integrity defines the number of rays cast from an illuminated surface. This parameter is not available if raytracing mode is simple. **Shadow Quality** defines the secondary rays cast from the illuminated surface. This parameter is not available when type is set to **Simple** or **1-Pass Antialias**. **Shadow Spread** defines the radius in pixels to blur the antialias edge. This parameter is not available when mode is set to **Simple**. **Shadow Bias** controls the minimum distance from the point being shaded that an object must be to cast a shadow. If you increase the blur value, you should also increase the bias value to compensate. The **Jitter Amount** parameters breaks the regular pattern of the rays and add randomness to the ray positions.

Area Shadows Rollout
This rollout is displayed when you choose the **Area Shadows** method for generating shadows. You need to define the dimensions of the virtual light to fake an area shadow. You can choose the type of fake light from the drop-down available in the **Basic Options** group of the rollout. The dimensions can be set from the **Area Light Dimensions** area of the rollout.

Tip: Rendering area lights
*If you are using area lights, try to match the properties of the light match the properties in the **Area Light Dimensions** section.*

Optimizations Rollout
This rollout contains additional parameters for fine tuning advanced raytraced and area shadows. When the **On** switch in the **Transparent Shadows** area is on, the transparent surfaces will cast a colored shadow, otherwise, all shadows are black. **Antialiasing Threshold** defines the maximum color difference allowed between transparent object samples before the antialiasing is triggered. On increasing the value of the color, the shadow becomes less sensitive to the aliasing artifacts and rendering speed will also improve. When the **Supersampled Material** switch is on, while shading a supersampled material only pass 1 is used during 2-pass antialiasing. When the **Reflect/Refract** switch is on, only pass 1 is used during 2-pass antialiasing. If these two switches are off, render time can increase without resulting in a better quality image.

The **Skip Coplanar Faces** switch in the **Coplanar Face Culling** group prevents faces from shadowing each other in curved surfaces. The angle between the adjacent faces is controlled by the **Threshold** parameter.

Target Directional Light
This light is used to simulate a distant light source [see Figure F14] that casts parallel light rays in a single direction [like Sun]. These lights are generally used to simulate sunlight. Like the **Target Spotlight**, it has a target object to aim the light. When you create a **Target Directional** light, the **Directional Parameters** appears in the **Modify** panel. You can use the parameters to define the shape of the light. These parameters are similar to the one described in the **Target Spotlight** section.

F14

Note: Free Directional Light

*The **Free Directional** light is similar to the **Target Directional** light except the difference that it has no target. You can move and rotate the **Free Directional** to aim in any direction.*

Omni Light

An **Omni** light casts rays in all directions from a single source like a light bulb. These lights are specifically used for creating fill lighting or simulating point source lights.

Skylight

When you use this light, it models a sky as a dome above the scene. You can use this light to model daylight. You can also use a map to model the sky. When you add a **Sky** light to the scene, the **Skylight Parameters** appear in the **Modify** panel.

The **On** switch allows you to turn light on or off. The **Multiplier** parameter controls the power of the light. The parameters in the **Sky Color** group let you set the color of the sky. Select **Use Scene Environment** to color the light using the environment color set in the **Environment** dialog. The **Sky Color** parameter lets you set a color tint for the sky. You can also assign a map using the **Map** switch. Use HDR files such as **OpenEXR** for best results.

Turn on the **Cast Shadow** switch in the **Render** section to cause the **Sky light** to cast shadows. Figure F15 show a teapot rendered with a skylight. The **Rays Per Sample** parameter allows you to set the number of rays used to calculate the skylight falling on a point in question. The **Ray Bias** parameter defines the closest distance at which objects can cast shadows on a given point in the scene.

F15

Note: Radiosity and Light Tracer

*The **Cast Shadows** switch has no effect when you are using **Radiosity** or **Light Tracer**. Also, the **Sky** light does not cast shadows in the **ActiveShader** rendering.*

Note: The Render group

*The parameters in this group are not available if you are not using the **Scanline** renderer or the **Light Tracer** is active.*

Tip: Sky light and Light Tracer

*There are many methods in 3ds Max to model the skylight. For best results, use the **Sky light** with **Light Tracer**.*

Note: Light Tracer

*The **Light Tracer** is a lighting plugin that is used to generate soft-edged shadows in a brightly lit scene such as outdoor scenes. It is typically used with the **Sky** light. It does not attempt to create a physically accurate lighting and it is easy to setup.*

Note: Radiosity

*It is a rendering technique used to calculate the indirect light in a scene. It calculates the inter-reflections of the diffuse light and then illuminates the scene. You can find the **Light Tracer** and **Radiosity** options in the **Advanced Lighting** panel of the **Render Setup** dialog.*

Hands-On Exercises

From the **Application** menu, choose **Manage | Set Project Folder** to open the **Browse for Folder** dialog. Navigate to a folder where you want to save the files and then click **Make New Folder**. Create the new folder with the name **unit-ml1** and click **OK** to create the project directory.

Exercise 1: Illuminating an Outdoor Scene

In this exercise, we are going to illuminate an outdoor scene using **Standard** lights. We will also use **Light Tracer** to enhance the scene [see Figure E1].

The following table summarizes the exercise.

Table E1: Illuminating an outdoor scene	
Skill Level	Beginner
Time to Complete	45 Minutes
Topics in this section:	• Getting Ready • Adding Lights to the scene • Enabling the **LightTracer** plugin • Changing the **Scanline** renderer filter settings
Project Folder	**unit-ml1**
Start File	**uml1-hoe1-start.max**
Final Exercise File	**uml1-hoe1-finish.max**

Getting Ready

Open the **uml1-hoe1-start.max** file in 3ds Max.

Adding Lights to the Scene

You will first add a directional light to simulate the light coming from Sun and then the **Skylight** light to model the light coming from the sky. On the **Create** panel, click **Lights** and then select **Standard** from the drop-down available below **Lights**. On the **Object Type** rollout, click **Target Direct** and then in the **Left** viewport click on the upper-left area of the viewport to place the light and then drag toward the ladder to aim the light. Now, release the mouse button to set the aim [see Figure E2].

On the **Modify** panel | **General Parameters** rollout, turn on the **On** switch from the **Shadows** section and then select **Adv. Ray Traced** option from the drop-down in this group. On the **Directional Parameters** rollout, set **Hotspot/Beam** to **17.58** so that the directional light covers the whole scene [see Figure E3]. Ensure the **Perspective** view is active and then press **C** to activate the **Camera** view. Render the scene [see Figure E4].

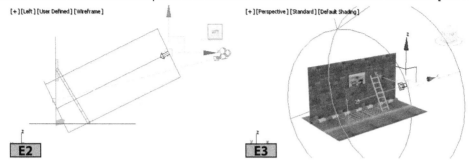

Now, you will add a **Skylight** to the scene. This light will provide the skylight and also it will create nice contact shadows. But, before we add the **Skylight**, let's turn off the directional light so that we can see what effect the **Skylight** produces. In the **General Parameters** rollout, turn off the **On** switch in the **Light Type** group.

On the **Create** panel | **Object Type** rollout, click **Skylight** and then click anywhere in the scene to place the **Skylight** in the scene. The position of the **Skylight** does not affect the way it illuminates the scene therefore you can place light anywhere in the scene. Render the scene. You will notice that 3ds Max rendered a washed out image [see Figure E5]. Let's adjust some parameters to get the effect correct.

On the **Modify** panel | **Skylight Parameters** rollout, set **Multiplier** to **0.3**, **Sky Color** to light blue color, **RGB [189, 192, 201]**. On the **Render** group, turn on the **Cast Shadows** switch and then set **Rays per Sample** to **10**. Render the scene [see Figure E6]. Notice that now we have got the better result.

Select the directional light from **Scene Explorer** and then turn it back on. On the **Intensity/Color/Attenuation** rollout, set color to a warm color, **RGB [255, 234, 197]**. Render the scene [see Figure E7]; notice the render is looking much better now after both the lights in the scene illuminates the objects in it. On the **Shadow Parameters** rollout, turn on the **Light Affects Shadow Color** switch.

Enabling Light Tracer

Open the **Render Setup** dialog and then go to **Advanced Lighting** panel. Select **Light Tracer** from the drop-down available in the **Select Advanced Lighting** rollout. Notice that the **Parameters** rollout appears in the panel. You can use the parameters available in this rollout to control the effect of the **Light Tracer** plugin.

On the **General Settings** group, set **Rays/Sample** to **500**, **Filter Size** to **0.7**, and **Bounce** to **1**. Now, render the scene to see the final render [see Figure E8]. Now, save the render as a 16 bit TIF file and farther refine the render in Photoshop. As you have seen **Light Tracer** allows you to create soft-shadows and also helps in producing a smooth render. Table E1.1 summarizes the **Light Tracer** parameters.

Table E1.1: The **Light Tracer** parameters

Parameter	Description
Global Multiplier	It defines the overall lighting level.
Object Multi.	It defines the level of the light reflected by the objects in the scene. The effect of this parameter is more pronounced when **Bounces** is set to a value of **2** or higher.
Sky Lights	It scales the intensity of the skylights.
Color Bleed	Defines the color bleed that happens when light is inter-reflected among the scene objects.
Rays/Sample	Defines the number of rays per sample used by **Light Tracer**. Increasing this value produces smooth results at a cost of render time.
Color Filter	It filter all the light falling on the object. Change color to apply a tint to the scene.
Filter Size	The filter size used to reduce the noise.
Extra Ambient	The color you set for this parameter [other than black], **Light Tracer** adds that extra color to the ambient.
Ray Bias	It controls the position of the bounced light effects.
Bounces	Defines the number of time a ray bounces. On increasing its value, the color bleed also increases in the scene. Higher the value, more light will flow in the scene, and better result **Light Tracer** will produce at a cost of render time.
Cone Angle	It controls the angle used for regathering.
Volumes	When this switch is on, **Light Tracer** multiplies the amount of light it gathers from the volumetric lighting effects.

The controls in the **Adaptive Undersampling** section let you speed up your renderings. These controls allow you to specify the settings to reduce the number of light samples taken. **Light Tracer** initially takes samples from a grid superimposed on the pixels of the scene. When it finds enough contrast between the samples, it subdivide that region and takes farther samples, down to a minimum area specified by the **Subdivide Down To** parameter.

If you are rendering a complex scene, **Light Tracer** can slow down the rendering. For test renderings or a quick preview, given below are some tips:

- To generate a quick render, lower the values for the **Rays/Sample** and **Filter Size** parameters.
- Use **Adaptive Undersampling** to create a quick preview. Set the **Initial Sample Spacing** and the **Subdivide Down To** settings to the same value and then lower the **Rays/Sample** value and set **Bounced** to 0.
- If there are some objects in the scene that have negligible impact on the scene, disable **Light Tracing** from these objects from the **Object Properties** dialog.
- To increase the amount of color bleeding, adjust the values of the **Bounces** and **Color Bleed** controls.
- If there are glass objects in the scene, increase the value for the **Bounces** parameter.
- If **Skylight** is the main light in the scene and you need specular highlights, create a directional light parallel to the **Skylight**. Turn on shadows for the light and turn off the **Diffuse** switch in the **Advanced Effects** rollout of the light. In the render shown in Figure E9, I have switched off the **Diffuse** switch for the directional light to create an overcast sky like effect [see **uml1-hoe1-overcast.max**].

Tip: Using map with the Skylight
*If you are using a map for the skylight, ensure that you completely blur the image in a program like Photoshop. You can blur the map beyond recognition and **Light Tracer** will still fetch the info required for gathering light. Blurring the image helps in reducing the render time. In the render shown in Figure E10, I have completely blurred the image and then applied to the **Skylight**. I have also set the contribution of the map to **30%** using the control on the right of the **Map** switch in the **Skylight Parameters** rollout [see **uml1-hoe1-blurredSky.max**].*

Exercise 2: Quickly Rendering an Architectural Plan
Sometimes, you need to send a quick draft render to your clients to check the CG assets and other related information in an architectural plan. Once approved, you can then proceed to produce the high quality render in **VRay**, or **Arnold**. In this exercise, we are going to render an architectural plan using the **Standard** lights and the **Light Tracer** plugin [see Figure E1]. To speed up the rendering, I have not placed any models in the scene except the walls.

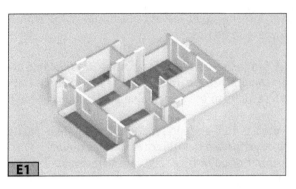

E1

Table E2 summarizes the exercise.

Table E2: Quickly rendering an architectural plan	
Skill Level	Intermediate
Time to Complete	30 Minutes
Topics in this section:	• Getting Ready • Illuminating the Plan
Project Folder	**unit-ml1**
Start File	**uml1-hoe2-start.max**
Final Exercise File	**uml1-hoe2-finish.max**

Getting Ready

Open the **uml1-hoe2-start.max** file in 3ds Max.

Illuminating the Plan

Add a **Skylight** to the scene and then in the **Modify** panel | **Skylight Parameters** rollout, set **Multiplier** to **0.5** and **Sky Color** to **RGB [184, 184, 255]**. Turn on the **Cast Shadows** switch in the **Render** section and then set **Rays per sample** to **10**. In the **Top** viewport, create a **Target Direct** light aiming toward the **Camera's** target. Now, in the **Left** viewport move the light up. You can use the following values for placing the light and its target: **Light [11825, -7069, 76]**, and **Target [11889, -7097, 0]**.

Now, change the parameters of the directional light in the **Modify** panel, refer to Table E2.1. Figure E2 shows the light in the scene. Now, make sure the **Camera** view is active and then render the scene [see Figure E3].

Table E2.1: The parameters of the **Target Light**	
Rollout	**Values**
General Parameters	Shadows	Turn on the **On** switch. Select **Adv. Ray Traced** shadows type.
Directional Parameters	Hotspot/Beam: **72**
Intensity/Color/Attenuation	Multiplier: **1.5**, Color: **RGB [255, 242, and 198]**.

Table E2.1: The parameters of the **Target Light**	
Rollout	**Values**
Shadow Parameters	Dens: **0.5**. Turn on the **Light Affects Shadow Color** switch.
Adv. Ray Traced Params	Shadow Integrity: **10**, Shadow Quality: **5**, Shadow Spread: **20**, and Jitter Amount: **0.8**

Enable **Light Tracing** from the **Render Setup dialog | Advanced Lighting** panel and then render the scene [see Figure E4].

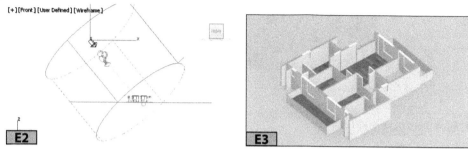

Adjust the **Light Tracer's** parameters using the values shown in Table E2.2.

Table E2.2: The parameters of the **Light Tracer**	
Rollout	**Values**
Parameters	Global Multiplier: **1.2**, Rays/Sample: **500**, Bounces: **2**
Parameters	Adaptive Undersampling	Initial Sampling Spacing: **32x32**

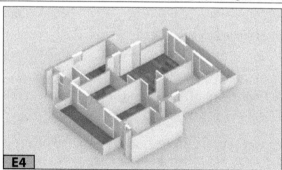

Now, render the scene [see Figure E1]. Experiment with various parameters of **Direct Light** and **Light Tracer** to achieve a different result.

Exercise 3: Illuminating a Night Scene

Here, we are going to illuminate the same scene that we used in Exercise 1 but here we will simulate night lighting by using the **Target Spot** and **Omni** lights [see Figure E1].

Table E3 summarizes the exercise.

Table E3: Illuminating a Night Scene	
Skill Level	Intermediate
Time to Complete	30 Minutes
Topics in this section:	• Getting Ready • Illuminating the Scene
Project Folder	**unit-ml1**
Start File	**uml1-hoe3-start.max**
Final Exercise File	**uml1-hoe3-finish.max**

Getting Ready

Open the **uml1-hoe3-start.max** file in 3ds Max.

Illuminating the Scene

Create a **Target Spot** light in the **Front** viewport and then align it [see Figure E2]. Now, select **Spot001** from **Scene Explorer**. In the **Front** viewport, drag the light with **Shift** held down along the X direction to the other light fixture on the left.

In the **Clone Options** dialog that appears, select **Instance** from the **Object** group and then click **OK** to create a clone of the selected light. Now, align the cloned light with the fixture [see Figure E3].

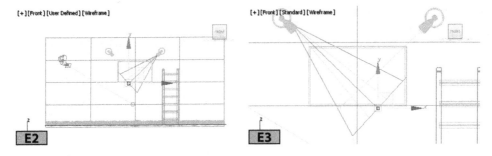

You can also use the values shown in Table E3.1 to position the spot lights.

Table E3.1: The transform values for spot lights	
Object	**XYZ Values**
Spot001	**39.991, -6.159, 116.401**
Spot001.Target	**-20.628, -6.159, 58.77**
Spot002	**-38.549, -6.159, 116.401**
Spot002.Target	**8.85, -6.159, 58.77**

Now, render the scene. You will notice [see Figure E4] that spot lights are illuminating the road as well. We need to confine the illumination to the billboard only. For that, we will use the **Attenuation** settings. Ensure a spot light is selected and then in the **Modify** panel | **Spotlight Parameters** rollout, set **Hotspot/Beam** to **43.7** and **Falloff/Field** to **67**. In the **Intensity/Color/Attenuation** | **Far Attenuation** section, turn on the **Use** and **Show** switches and then set **End** to **116**. Now, render the scene to see the area the spotlights are illuminating [see Figure E5].

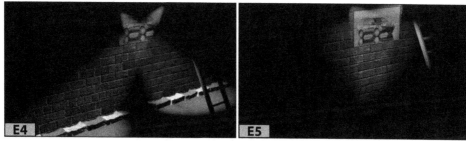

Now, add an **Omni** light to the scene and place it at the following location [XYZ]: **38.169, -103.246, 117.664**. Change the parameters of the **Omni** light using the values shown in Table E3.2 and then render the scene [see Figure E6].

Table E3.2: The parameters of the **Omni** light	
Rollout	**Values**
General Parameters	Shadows	Turn on the **On** switch. Select **Adv. Ray Traced** shadows type.
Intensity/Color/Attenuation	Multiplier: **0.1**, Color: **RGB [173, 175, and 208]**.

Table E3.2: The parameters of the **Omni** light	
Rollout	**Values**
Shadow Parameters	Turn on the **Light Affects Shadow Color** switch.
Adv. Ray Traced Params	Shadow Integrity: **10**, Shadow Quality: **5**, Shadow Spread: **10**, and Jitter Amount: **0.7**

In the **Modify** panel | **Intensity/Color/Attenuation** rollout of a spot light, set **Multiplier** to **2** to make the area illuminated by the spot lights brighter. Render the scene to view the result.

Quiz
Evaluate your skills to see how many questions you can answer correctly.

Multiple Choice
Answer the following questions, only one choice is correct.

1. Which of the following options are available for controlling the decay of the light?

    [A] **None**   [B] **Inverse**
    [C] **Inverse Square**   [D] All of the above

2. Which of the following algorithms are available for controlling shadows?

    [A] **Ray-Traced**   [B] **Area**
    [C] **Shadow Map**   [D] All of the above

Fill in the Blanks
Fill in the blanks in each of the following statements:

1. _____ is a bitmap that is generated during a pre-rendering pass of the scene.

2. The _____ shadows are more accurate than the shadow-mapped shadows and are generated by tracing the path of the rays sampled from a light source.

3. The _____ formula is used to calculate the **Inverse** decay type. _____ is the radial source of the light of no attenuation is used. _____ is the radial distance of the illuminated surface from _____ .

4. The _____ switch displays the cone of a spot light in the viewport.

5. The _____ control moves the shadow toward or away from the shadow casting object.

6. An _____ light casts rays in all directions from a single source like a light bulb.

True or False

State whether each of the following is true or false:

1. The **Standard** lights have physically-based intensity values.

2. The color that you set for the light from the **Name and Color** rollout only changes the color of the light geometry in the scene. It has no effect on the color cast by the light.

3. When you delete all light objects from the scene, 3ds Max uses the default lighting for illuminating the scene.

4. **Free Spotlight** is similar to **Target Spotlight** except the difference that it has no target.

5. Only ray-traced shadows can generate shadows for the wireframed objects.

6. You cannot prevent an object from casting shadows in the scene.

7. When the **Overshoot** switch is on for a spot light, the light casts light in all directions [not just within the cone] but the shadows and projections appear within the cone.

Summary
This unit covered the following topics:

*   Basic Lighting Concepts
*   3ds Max Lights
*   Light Linking
*   Shadows
*   Lighting Effects

Unit ML2: Photometric Lights

Photometric lights allow you to accurately define the lighting model for your scene. They use the light energy [**Photometric values, real-world light measurement values**] to create lights that follow the real-world scenarios. You can create lighting models using various distribution and color characteristics. You can also import photometric light files [provided by the light manufactures] into 3ds Max. In this unit, you will learn about photometric lights that 3ds Max offers.

In this unit, I will describe the following:

- Photometric light types: **Target Light**, and **Free Light**
- Color temperatures
- Shadow generating shapes
- Exposure controls

Target Light

Target Light has a target sub-object that you can use to aim the light. When you create **Target Light** in a viewport, 3ds Max automatically adds a **Look At Controller** to it. The target object of the light is assigned as **Look At Target**. You can use the **Motion** panel of **Command Panel** to assign any object as the **Look At Target**.

Note: Light and its target

*When you create a light that has a target, two objects will appear in **Scene Explorer**: light object and its target. The target name has an extension **.target**. For example, if you create first **Target Light** in the scene, the name of the light and its target will be as follows: **TPhotometricLight001**and **TPhotometricLight001.Target**. When you rename a light, its target object will be automatically renamed accordingly. However, remember that renaming a target object does not rename its parent light.*

Whenever you create a photometric light, a message box appears, recommending that the **Logarithmic Exposure Control** to be enabled. Exposure controls are plug-in components that are used to adjust the output levels and color range of a rendering as if you are adjusting the film exposure [tone mapping]. These controls are useful if you are rendering a scene with **Radiosity** or **HDR** imagery. It is especially useful for compensating the limited dynamic range of the computer displays. The following table summarizes the exposure controls available in 3ds Max.

Table 1: Exposure Controls	
Control	**Description**
Automatic Exposure Control	This control enhances some lighting effects that would otherwise be too dim to see. It builds a histogram to give good color separation across the entire dynamic range of the rendering. Do not use this control in animation because it causes the animation to flicker. This happens because different histograms are generated for each frame.

Table 1: Exposure Controls	
Control	**Description**
Linear Exposure Control	It uses the average brightness of the scene to map physical values to the RGB values. This is best suitable for scene with fairly low dynamic range.
Logarithmic Exposure Control	It uses brightness and contrast to map physical values to RGB values. This control is best suitable for scenes with a very high dynamic range. Also, it is best suited for animation as it does not generate histograms. If you're rendering to texture, use the **Logarithmic Exposure Control**, not the **Automatic** or **Linear** control.
Physical Camera Exposure Control	It sets exposure for **Physical Cameras**, using an **Exposure Value** and a color-response curve.
Pseudo Color Exposure Control	It is a lighting analysis tool that provides an intuitive way of visualizing and evaluating the lighting levels in the scenes.

To create a target light, on the **Create** panel, click **Lights** and then choose **Photometric** from the drop-down [see Figure F1]. Click **Target Light** in the **Object Type** rollout. Click **Yes** from the **Photometric Light Creation** message box and then drag in a viewport to set the location of the light. The initial point drag of the mouse pointer defines the location of the light whereas the last drag point defines the position of the target. Now, you can use the **Move** transform to farther refine the position of the light and its target. Adjust the parameters of the light from the rollouts in **Command Panel**.

Several of the rollouts for the photometric lights are the same as those for the standard lights but there are some key controls that are different. Let's now explore these controls.

Template Rollout
This rollout [see Figure F2] allows you to choose a light preset among a variety of preset light types. When you choose a template from this rollout, the parameters in other rollouts updated that you can use to fine-tune the settings of the light.

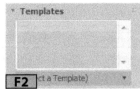

The following presets are available in the **Template** rollout:

(Bulb Lights)
- 40 Watt (W) Bulb
- 60W Bulb
- 75W Bulb
- 100W Bulb

(Halogen Lights)
- Halogen Spotlight
- 21W Halogen Bulb
- 35W Halogen Bulb
- 50W Halogen Bulb
- 75W Halogen Bulb
- 80W Halogen Bulb
- 100W Halogen Bulb

(Recessed Lights)

- Recessed 75W Lamp (web)
- Recessed 75W Wallwash (web)
- Recessed 250W Wallwash (web)

(Fluorescent Lights)
- 4 ft. Pendant Fluorescent (web)
- 4 ft. Cove Fluorescent (web)

(Other Lights)
- Street 400W Lamp (web)
- Stadium 1000W Lamp (web)

General Parameters Rollout

The parameters in this rollout are similar to that of the standard lights that we saw in **Unit ML1** except the **Light Distribution (Type)** group. The drop-down in this group lets you choose the type of the light distribution model. The model defines the method of how a photometric light is distributed. Let's explore these types.

- **Uniform Spherical:** This type casts lights in all directions [see Figure F3] like the standard **Omni** light. The **Uniform** distribution is represented by a small sphere in the viewports. The position of the sphere indicates whether the distribution is spherical or hemispherical.

- **Uniform Diffuse:** This type casts diffuse light in one hemisphere [as if a light is positioned along a wall] only according to the **Lambert's** cosine law [see Figure F4].

- **Spotlight Distribution:** This type casts a focused beam of light [see Figure F5] like a flashlight or a car's headlights. The beam angle of the light defines the main strength of the beam whereas the field angle defines the spill of the light.

- **Photometric Web:** A photometric web is based on a geometric web that represents the light intensity distribution of a light source [see Figure F5]. The distribution information is stored in a photometric data file [that can be obtained from the light's manufacturer] in the **IES** format using the **IES LM-63-1991** standard file format.

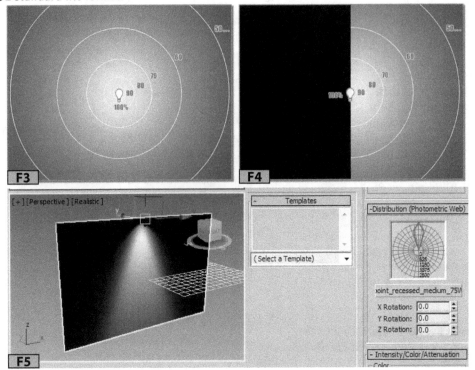

Intensity/Color/Attenuation Rollout

This rollout [see Figure F6] lets you set the color and intensity of the light. You can also set attenuation form this rollout.

Color Group

The first drop-down in this group allows you to pick a common lamp specification. Given below are the options available:

- D50 Illuminant (Reference White)
- D65 Illuminant (Reference White) (the default)
- Fluorescent (Cool White)
- Fluorescent (Daylight)
- Fluorescent (Lite White)
- Fluorescent (Warm White)
- Fluorescent (White)
- Halogen
- Halogen (Cool)
- Halogen (Warm)

- HID Ceramic Metal Halide (Cool)
- HID Ceramic Metal Halide (Warm)
- HID High Pressure Sodium
- HID Low Pressure Sodium
- HID Mercury
- HID Phosphor Mercury
- HID Quartz Metal Halide
- HID Quartz Metal Halide (Cool)
- HID Quartz Metal Halide (Warm)
- HID Xenon
- Incandescent filament lamp

Note: HID

HID stands for high–intensity discharge.

Note: D65 Illuminant (Reference White)

The default option in the drop–down approximates a mid day sun in western or northern Europe. **D65** is a white value defined by the **Comission Internationale de l'Éclairage (CIE)**, the **International Lighting Commission**.

Figure F7 shows the render with the **D50 Illuminant (Reference White)**, **Fluorescent (Cool White)**, and **HID High Pressure Sodium**, respectively.

In addition to the list of lights, you can specify a color based on the temperature expressed in **Kelvin**. The **Kelvin** option allows you to set the color of the light by adjusting the color temperature spinners located next to it. The associated color appears on the color swatch on the right of the spinner. **Filter Color** allows you to simulate the effect of a color filter placed in front of the light source. The color temperature defines a color in terms of degree **Kelvin [K]**. The following table summarizes the color temperature for some common types of lights:

Table 2: Color Temperatures		
Light Source	**Temperature [K]**	**Hue**
Overcast daylight	6000	130
Noontime sunlight	5000	58
White fluorescent	4000	27
Tungsten/halogen lamp	3300	20
Incandescent lamp (100 to 200 W)	2900	16

Table 2: Color Temperatures		
Light Source	**Temperature [K]**	**Hue**
Incandescent lamp (25 W)	2500	12
Sunlight at sunset or sunrise	2000	7
Candle flame	1750	5

Intensity Group

There are three controls in this group: **lm** [lumen], **cd** [candela], and **lx at** [lux]. These controls define the strength or brightness of the lights in physically based quantities. **Lumen** measures the overall output [luminous flux] power of the light. A **100 watt** bulb has about **1750 lm** luminous flux. **Candela** measures the maximum luminous intensity of the light, generally along the direction of the aim. A **100 watt** bulb has about intensity of **139 cd**. **Lux** measures the illuminate caused by the light shining on a surface at a certain distance in the direction of the source. **Lux** is the international scene unit and which is equivalent to **1 lumen per square meter**. To specify the illuminate of the light first enter the **lx** value in the first spinner and then enter **distance** in the second.

Dimming Group

The **Resulting Intensity** label shows the intensity caused by the dimming. It uses the same units that you have defined in the **Intensity** group. Turn on the **Dimming Percentage** switch to control the dimming of the light. At **100%**, the light has full intensity. When the **Incandescent lamp color shift when dimming** switch is on, the light simulate an incandescent light. The color of the light turns more yellowish as it is dimmed.

Shape/Area Shadows Rollout

You can use the parameters in this rollout [see Figure F8] to choose the light shape used for generating shadows. Let's explore the parameters.

Emit Light From (Shape) Group

The drop-down in this group allows you to choose the shadow generating shape for the light. When you choose a shadow generating shape other than **Point**, the parameters appear in the **Emit Light From** section to control the dimensions of the shape. Also, the **Shadow Samples** control appears in the **Rendering** section of the rollout.

The following table summarizes the shapes.

Table 3: Shadow Generating Shapes	
Shape	**Description**
Point	Calculates shadows as if the light were emitted from a point like a light bulb. It has no other controls.
Line	Calculates shadows as if the light were emitted from a line like a fluorescent tube. This shape has a length control.

Table 3: Shadow Generating Shapes	
Shape	**Description**
Rectangle	Calculates shadows as if the light were emitted from a rectangular area like a bank of fluorescent lights. This shape has length and width controls.
Disc	Calculates shadows as if the light were emitted from a disc like the light out of the top of a shaded lamp. This shape has radius control.
Sphere	Calculates shadows as if the light were emitted from a sphere like a Chinese lantern. This shape has radius control.
Cylinder	Calculates shadows as if the light were emitted from a cylinder. This shape has length and radius controls.

Rendering Group

When the **Light Shape Visible in Rendering** switch is on, the shape is visible in the renderings as a self-illuminated glowing shape. When switch is off, no shape is rendered. The **Shadow Samples** drop-down sets the overall quality of the shadows for the lights that have an area. If the render is grainy, increase the value for the **Shadow Samples** control. This setting does not appear for the **Point** shadow shape.

Distribution (Photometric File) Rollout

This rollout appears [see Figure F9] when you create or select a light with a photometric web distribution. You can use the controls in this rollout to select a photometric web file and adjust its parameters. After you choose a photometric file, the thumbnail [also referred to as **Web Diagram**] shows a schematic diagram of the distribution pattern of the light [see Figure F5].

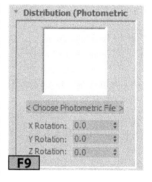

The bright red outline shows the beam of the light. In some web diagrams, you will see a darker red outline that shows the field which is less bright than the beam. Click **Choose Photometric File** to select a file to use as a photometric web. The file can be in one of the following formats: **IES**, **LTLI**, or **CIBSE**. Once you select the file, this button displays the name of the file. The **X Rotation**, **Y Rotation**, and **Z Rotation** controls rotate the web about the **X**, **Y**, and **Z** axis, respectively.

Distribution (Spotlight) Rollout

This rollout appears [see Figure F10] when you select or create a photometric light with the spotlight distribution. The parameters in this rollout control hotspots and falloff of the spotlights. Use the **Hotspot/Beam** and **Falloff/Field** controls to increase or decrease the size of the beam angle and field angle regions. The **Cone visible in viewport when unselected** switch toggles the display of the cone on or off.

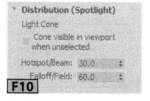

Free Light

The **Free Light** is similar to **Target Light** except it has no target sub-object.

Quiz

Evaluate your skills to see how many questions you can answer correctly.

Multiple Choice

Answer the following questions, only one choice is correct.

1. Which of the following exposure controls is used with the **Photometric** lights?

   [A] **Linear Exposure Control**   [B] **Logarithmic Exposure Control**
   [C] **Physical Camera Exposure Control** [D] All of the above

2. Which of the following light distribution models are available for the **Photometric** lights?

   [A] **Uniform Spherical**   [B] **Uniform Diffuse**
   [C] **Photometric Web**   [D] All of the above

3. Which of the following file types can be used to assign web diagrams to the **Photometric** lights?

   [A] **IES**   [B] **CIBSE**
   [C] **LTLI**   [D] All of the above

Fill in the Blanks

Fill in the blanks in each of the following statements:

1. When you create **Target Light** in a viewport, 3ds Max automatically adds a _____ to it.

2. _____ controls are plug-in components that are used to adjust the output levels and color range of a rendering as if you are adjusting the film exposure [tone mapping].

3. _____ stands for high-intensity discharge.

True or False

State whether each of the following is true or false:

1. **Physical Camera Exposure Control** sets exposure for **Physical** cameras, using an **Exposure Value** and a color-response curve.

2. The **Resulting Intensity** label shows the intensity caused by the dimming.

Summary

This units covered the following topics:

- Photometric light types: **Target Light**, and **Free Light**
- Color temperatures
- Shadow generating shapes
- Exposure controls

Unit ML3: Sunlight and Daylight Systems

The sunlight and daylight systems are the built for simulating external lighting based on the Sun. These systems follow the geographically correct angle and movement of the sun over the earth at a given location and are suitable for shadow study for proposed or existing structures. Using these systems, you can animate date and time, latitude, longitude, **North Direction** [rotational direction of the compass rose], and **Orbital Scale** [the distance of the sun from the ground plane].

In this unit, I will describe the following:

- **Sunlight** and **Daylight** Systems
- Positioning the Compass
- Choosing a location
- **Sun Positioner** and **Physical Sky**

Using the Sunlight and Daylight Systems

The legacy **Sunlight** and **Daylight** systems are similar in how they are used [they have similar interface] but there are some differences:

- **Sunlight** uses a directional light.
- **Daylight** combines **Sunlight** and **Skylight**. The **Sunlight** component can be one of the following: **IES Sun** light or a standard light (a target direct light). The **Skylight** component can be one of the following: **IES Sky** light or a **Skylight**.

Note: Standard and Photometric Lights

*The **IES Sun** and **IES Sky** lights are photometric lights. You can use them if you are rendering a scene using **Radiosity** and exposure control. The **Standard** light and **Skylight** are non-photometric. You can use them if you are using standard lighting or you are using light tracing.*

You can access the **Sunlight** and **Daylight** systems from the **System** panel of the **Command Panel**. To create either of these systems, go to the **Create** panel and then click **Systems** [see Figure F1]. On the **Object Type** rollout, click **Sunlight** or **Daylight** and drag the mouse pointer in a viewport [should be **Top**, **Perspective**, or **Camera** view].

A compass helper object appears on the grid. Click again to create a **Direct** light representing the sun and drag to set its height above the ground plane. Figure F2 shows the compass created using the **Daylight** system.

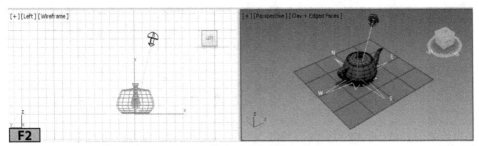

When you first create a **Daylight** system, the **Daylight System Creation** message box appears [see Figure F3], recommending to enable the **Logarithmic Exposure Control** for external light. Click **Yes** to enable the exposure control.

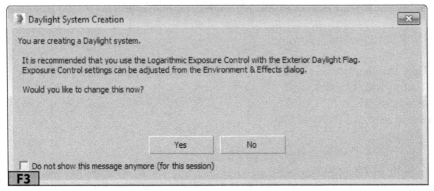

Upon creation, you will have two objects in the scene. The compass rose, which is a helper object and provides the world directions for the sun. The light itself which is child of the compass and is always targeted at the center of the compass rose. If you have created a **Daylight** system, you can choose the type of sunlight and skylight from the **Modify** panel. The **Sunlight** drop-down list lets you choose **IES Sun** or **Standard (directional)**. The **Skylight** drop-down list lets you choose **IES Sky** or **Skylight**. You can also choose <**No Sunlight**> or <**No Skylight**> from the drop-downs.

The controls for adjusting the geographic location of the sun can be accessed from the **Motion** panel of **Command Panel**. The default time is noon whereas the default date and time is dependent on the settings of the computer you are using. The default location is **San Francisco, CA**.

Once you create a **Daylight** system, the parameters appear in the **Modify** panel. Let's explore the parameters that are unique to the **Daylight** system:

Daylight Parameters Rollout

The controls in this rollout [see Figure F4] lets you define the sun object of the **Daylight** system. You can use these controls to set the behavior of the sunlight and skylight. The **Sunlight** drop-down lets you choose the sunlight for your scene. You can use one of the following options: **IES Sun, Standard**, and **No Sunlight**. The **Active** switch lets you toggle the sunlight on or off. The **Skylight** drop-down lets you choose the skylight for your scene. The available options are: **IES Sky, Skylight**, and **No Skylight**.

The controls in the **Position** section lets you define the correct geographical angle of the sun. The **Manual** control lets you manually adjust the location of the daylight. The **Date, Time and Location** control uses the geographically correct angle and movement of the sun over the earth at a given location. The **Weather Data File** control allows you to derive the angle and intensity of the sun from a weather data (**EPW**) file.

When you choose the **Weather Data File** and then click **Setup**, 3ds Max opens the **Configure Weather Data** dialog. You can choose which weather data you want the daylight system to use. When you choose the **Manual** or **Date, Time And Location** control, clicking on **Setup** button opens the **Motion** panel [see Figure F5] from where you can set the time, location, and site of your daylight system.

F5

Control Parameters Rollout

The **Azimuth** and **Altitude** controls display the azimuth and altitude of the sun. **Azimuth** is the compass direction [**North=0**, **East=90**] of the sun in degrees. **Altitude** is the height [**Sunrise/Sunset=0**] of the sun above the horizon in degrees. The controls in the **Time** group let you define the time, date, and time zone. When the **Daylight Savings Time** switch is on, 3ds Max calculates daylight savings by adjusting azimuth and altitude during the summer months.

The controls in **Location** group let you define location of your scene in the world. You can manually enter location based on the latitude and longitude. You can also specify location by using the **Geographic Location Dialog** which opens [see Figure F6] when you click **Get Location**. You can define the longitude and latitude values by selecting a location on the map or from a list of cities. The **North Direction** control sets the rotational direction of the compass rose in the scene. By default, north direction is **0**.

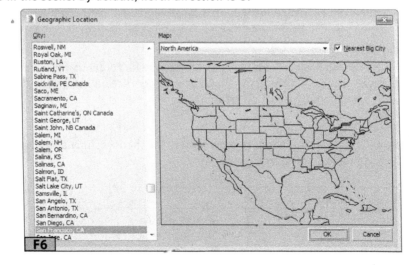

F6

The **Orbital Scale** control in the **Site** group defines the distance of the Sun from the compass rose. The distance of Sun from the compass rose has no effect on the accuracy of the sunlight.

Using Sun Positioner and Physical Sky

Like **Daylight** and **Sunlight** systems, the **Sun Positioner** and **Physical Sky** system provides the light follows the geographically correct angle and movement of the Sun over the earth at a given location. However, the **Sun Positioner** and **Physical Sky** system provides intuitive workflow compared to these legacy systems. The component of the legacy systems are scattered all over the interface. For example, the legacy systems are located in the **System** panel of **Command Panel** whereas the location settings are found in the **Motion** panel of **Command Panel**.

The **Sun Positioner/Physical Sky** system is found in the **Light** panel. Once you position the Sun object in the scene, you can adjust the exposure controls from the **Environment and Effects** window. The shading parameters can be adjusted from the **Scene Materials** rollout of **Material Editor** [see Figure F7].

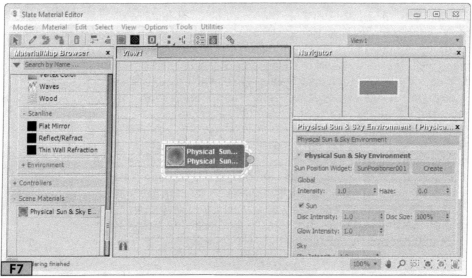

Hands-on Exercise

From the **File** menu, choose **Set Project Folder** to open the **Browse for Folder** dialog. Navigate to the folder where you want to save the files and then click **Make New Folder**. Create the new folder with the name **unit-ml3** and click **OK** to create the project directory.

Exercise 1: Shadow Pattern Study

In this exercise, we will create an animated shadow pattern for shadow study according to the position of the Sun. The following table summarizes the exercise.

Table E1: Shadow Pattern Study	
Topics in this section:	• Getting Ready • Creating the Gold Material
Skill Level	Intermediate

Table E1: Shadow Pattern Study	
Project Folder	**unit-ml3**
Start File	**uml3-hoe1-start.max**
Final Exercise File	**uml3-hoe1-end.max**
Time to Complete	25 Minutes

Getting Ready

Open the **uml3-hoe1-start.max** file in 3ds Max.

Creating the Gold Material

On the **Create** panel, click **Lights** and then select **Photometric** from the drop-down available below **Lights**. On the **Object Type** rollout, click **Sun Positioner** and then create a Sun Positioner object in the scene. Choose the **Time Configuration** button ⚙ from the timeline to open the **Time Configuration** dialog. In this dialog, set **End Time** to **500** and then click **OK**.

Make sure the **SunPositioner001** object is selected and time slider is at frame **0**. Switch to the **Modify** panel. On the **Display** rollout, set **Radius** to **0.987** and **North Offset** to **100**. On the **Sun** section, set **Distance** to **555.74**. Figure E1 shows the **SunPositioner001** object in the scene.

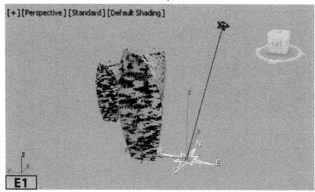

E1

The **SunPositioner001** object uses **San Francisco, CA** as the default location. If you want to change the location, click on **San Francisco, CA** from the **Location on Earth** section of the **Sun Position** rollout to open the **Geographic Location** dialog. Now, you can choose desired location from this dialog.

On the **Date & Time** section, turn off the **Use Date Range** switch and then set **Time** to **7:00**. Toggle on the **Auto Key** mode [Auto Key] from the timeline. Drag the time slide to frame **500**. On the **Date & Time** section of the **Sun Position** rollout, set **Time** to **18:00**. Toggle off the **Auto Key** mode and then click the **Play Animation** button ▶ to view the animation of Sun. Now, render the sequence to see the shadow pattern. Figure E2 shows the render at frame **25** and **80**, respectively.

Quiz

Evaluate your skills to see how many questions you can answer correctly.

Fill in the Blanks

Fill in the blanks in each of the following statements:

1. _____ uses a directional light to simulate the sun.

2. You can access the **Sunlight** and **Daylight** systems from the _____ panel of **Command Panel**.

3. If you have created a _____ system, you can choose the type of sunlight and skylight from the **Modify** panel.

4. The _____ system provides intuitive workflow than the legacy **Daylight** and **Sunlight** systems for the geographically correct angle and movement of the Sun over the earth at a given location.

Summary

This unit covered the following:

- **Sunlight** and **Daylight** Systems
- Positioning the Compass
- Choosing a location
- **Sun Positioner** and **Physical Sky**

Unit MBT - Bonus Hands-on Exercises

Before starting the exercises of this unit, let's first create the project folder. From the **File** menu, choose| **Set Project Folder** to open the **Browse for Folder** dialog. Navigate to the location where you want to save the file and then click **Make New Folder**. Create the new folder with the name **unit-mbt** and click **OK** to create the project directory.

Exercises - Texturing and Lighting

Exercise T1: Creating Balloon Material

In this exercise, we will create a balloon shader using the **Shellac** material.

The following table summarizes the exercise:

Table ET1 - Creating Balloon Material	
Skill level	Intermediate
Time to complete	20 Minutes
Topics in the section	• Getting Ready • Creating the Material
Project Folder	**unit-mbt**
Start File	**umbt-mat1-start.max**
Final exercise file	**umbt-hoet1-finish.max**

Getting Ready

Open the **umbt-mat1-start.max** file.

Creating the Material

Open **Slate Material Editor** and then drag the **Shellac** material to the active view. Rename the material as **balloonMat**. Apply material to **geo1**, **geo2**, and **geo3**. Rename the material connected to the **Shellac Mat** slot as **glossMat**. Similarly, rename the material connected to the **Base Material** slot as **colorFallOffMat**. First, we will create the glossy material and then we will model translucency for the material.

On the **Parameter Editor | glossMat | Blinn Basic Parameters** rollout, set **Diffuse** to **Red**. On the **Specular Highlights** section, set **Specular Level** and **Glossiness** to **225** and **70**, respectively. On the **Parameter Editor | Shellac Basic Parameters** rollout, set **Shellac Color Blend** to **30**.

On the **Parameter Editor | colorFallOffMat | Shader Basic Parameters** rollout, select **Translucent Shader** from the drop-down. Now, on the **Translucent Basic Parameters** rollout set **Diffuse** and **Specular** to **RGB [246, 14, 14]** and **RGB [235, 255, 141]**, respectively.

On the **Specular Highlights** section, set **Specular Level** and **Glossiness** to **99** and **22**, respectively. Render the scene [see Figure E1]. Notice that we have created a glossy red material. Now, we will add translucency to the material.

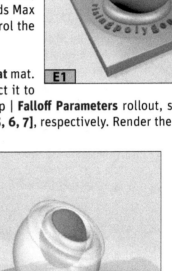

On the **Translucency** section, set **Translucent Clr**, **Filter Color**, and **Opacity** to **RGB [250, 143, 143]**, **RGB [221, 198, 148]**, and **30**, respectively. Render the scene [see Figure E2]. Notice that 3ds Max has added translucency to the material but we need to control the opacity as well the translucency based on the viewing angle.

Connect a **Falloff** map to the **Opacity** slot of the **colorFallOffMat** mat. Create a copy of the **Falloff** map using **Shift** and then connect it to **Translucent Color** node. On the **Property Editor | Falloff** map | **Falloff Parameters** rollout, set the first and second color swatches to **RGB [230, 87, 77]** and **RGB [55, 6, 7]**, respectively. Render the scene [see Figure E3].

Exercise T2: Creating Concrete Asphalt Material
In this exercise, we will create concrete asphalt material.

The following table summarizes the exercise:

Table ET2 - Creating Asphalt Material	
Skill level	Beginner
Time to complete	15 Minutes
Topics in the section	• Getting Ready • Creating the Material
Project Folder	**unit-mbt**
Start File	**umbt-mat1-start.max**
Final exercise file	**umbt-hoet2-finish.max**

Getting Ready

Open the **umbt-mat1-start.max** file.

Creating the Material

Open **Slate Material Editor** and then drag the **Standard** material to the active view. Rename the material as **asphaltMat**.

Apply material to **geo1**, **geo2**, and **geo3**. On the **Parameter Editor | asphaltMat | Blinn Basic Parameters** rollout, set **Ambient** to **RGB [25, 25, 25]**. On the **Specular Highlights** section, set **Specular Level** and **Glossiness** to **48** and **23**, respectively.

Connect **asphalt.bmp** to the **Diffuse Color** node of **asphaltMat**. Create copies of the bitmap node using **Shift** and connect them to **Specular Color**, **Specular Level**, and **Bump** nodes.

Render the scene [see Figure E1].

E1

Exercise T3: Creating Eyeball Material

In this exercises, we will create material for eyeball.

The following table summarizes the exercise:

Table ET3 - Creating Eyeball Material	
Skill level	Beginner
Time to complete	15 Minutes
Topics in the section	• Getting Ready • Creating the Material
Project Folder	**unit-mbt**
Start File	**umbt-mat2-start.max**
Final exercise file	**umbt-hoet3-finish.max**

Getting Ready

Open the **umbt-mat2-start.max** file.

Creating the Material

Open **Slate Material Editor** and then drag the **Raytrace** material to the active view. Rename the material as **eyeballMat**. Apply material to **GeoSphere001**. On the **Parameter Editor | eyeballMat | Raytrace Basic Parameters** rollout, set **Index of Refl** to **1.6**. On the **Specular Highlight** section, set **Specular Level** and **Glossiness** to **225** and **60**, respectively. Connect **eyeball.jpg** to the **Diffuse** slot of **eyeballMat**.

Connect a **Faloff** map to the **Reflect** slot of **eyeballMat**. On the **Falloff Parameters** rollout, set **Falloff Type** to **Fresnel**.

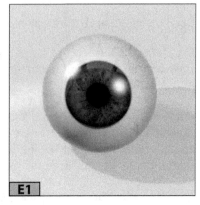

E1

Render the scene [see Figure E1].

Exercise T4: Creating Water Material

In this exercises, we will create the water material.

The following table summarizes the exercise:

Table ET4 - Creating Water Material	
Skill level	Beginner
Time to complete	15 Minutes
Topics in the section	• Getting Ready • Creating the Material
Project Folder	**unit-mbt**
Start File	**umbt-mat3-start.max**
Final exercise file	**umbt-hoet4-finish.max**

Getting Ready

Open the **umbt-mat3-start.max** file.

Creating the Material

Open **Slate Material Editor** and then drag the **Standard** material to the active view. Rename the material as **waterMat**. Apply material to **GeoSphere001**. On the **Parameter Editor | waterMat | Shader Basic Parameters** rollout, select **Anisotropic** from the drop-down. On the **Anisotropic Basic Parameters** rollout, set **Ambient** to **RGB [12, 12, 12]**, **Diffuse** to **RGB [85, 127, 157]**, and **Specular** to **RGB [160, 178, 190]**.

On the **Specular Highlight** section, set **Specular Level, Glossiness,** and **Anisotropy** to **160, 55,** and **60**, respectively. Connect **Noise** map to the **Bump** slot of **waterMat**. On the **Noise** map | **Noise Parameters** rollout, set **Noise Type** to **Fractal**, **Levels** to **9**, and **Size** to **18**.

E1

Connect **Mask** map to the **Reflection** slot of **waterMat**. Connect **lakerem.jpg** to the **Map** slot of the **Mask** map. On the **Parameter Editor | lakerem.jpg | Coordinates** rollout, select **Environ** and then set **Mapping** to **Spherical Environment**. Connect **Falloff** map to the **Mask** slot of the **Mask** map. On the **Property Editor | Falloff** map | **Falloff Parameters** rollout, set **Falloff Type** to **Fresnel**. Render the scene [see Figure E1].

Exercise T5: Creating X-Ray Material

In this exercises, we will create the X-Ray material.

The following table summarizes the exercise:

Table ET5 - Creating X-Ray Material	
Skill level	Intermediate
Time to complete	15 Minutes
Topics in the section	• Getting Ready • Creating the Material
Project Folder	**unit-mbt**
Start File	**umbt-mat1-start.max**
Final exercise file	**umbt-hoet5-finish.max**

Getting Ready

Open the **umbt-mat3-start.max** file.

Creating the Material

Open **Slate Material Editor** and then drag the **Standard** material to the active view. Rename the material as **xrayMat**. Apply material to **geo1**, **geo2**, and **geo3**. On the **Parameter Editor | xrayMat | Blinn Basic Parameters** rollout, set **Specular Level** and **Glossiness** to 0 and 10, respectively. Connect the **Falloff** map to the **Diffuse Color** slot of the **xrayMat**. On the **Property Editor | Falloff** map | **Mix Curve** rollout, shape the curve as shown in Figure E1. Now, connect the existing **Falloff** map to the **Self-illumination** and **Opacity** slots of **xrayMat**. Render the scene [see Figure E2].

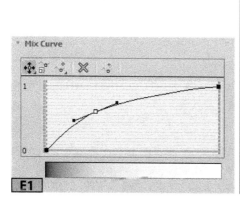

E1

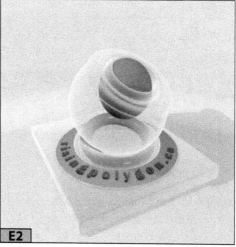

E2

Exercise T6: Texturing a Cardboard Box

In this exercise, we will texture a cardboard box [see Figure E1] using **UV Editor**.

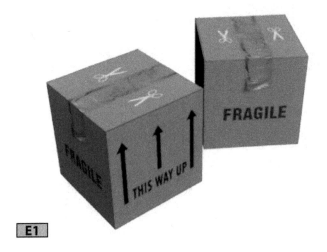

E1

The following Table summarizes the exercise.

Table ET6 - Texturing the Cardboard Box	
Skill level	Intermediate
Time to complete	20 Minutes
Topics in the section	• Getting Ready • Texturing the Cardboard Box
Project Folder	**unit-mbt**
Final exercise file	**umbt-hoet6-finish.max**

Getting Ready

Reset 3ds Max. Set units to **Generic Units** and then create a box with the **Length**, **Height**, and **Width** set to **190**.

Texturing the Cardboard Box

Ensure the box is selected in a viewport and then go to **Modify** panel. Add the **Unwrap UVW** modifier to the stack.

Note: Unwrap UVW Modifier

*This modifier allows you to assign texturing coordinates to objects and sub-object selections. You can edit the coordinates using various tools. You can use this modifier on Mesh, Patch, Polygon, HSDS, and NURBS meshes. This modifier gives you access to the **Edit UVWs** window which is a texture-coordinate editor. You can also use it along with the **UVW Map** modifier. This is required when you want to use a mapping method that is not available [such as **Shrink Wrap**] with the **Unwrap UVW** modifier.*

Note: UVW Map Modifier

The **UVW Map** modifier controls how mapped and procedural textures appear on the surface of the geometry. The UVW mapping coordinates are used to project bitmaps onto an object. This coordinate system is similar to the XYZ coordinate system. The **U** and **V** axes of a bitmap corresponds to the **X** and **Y** axes whereas the **W** axis corresponds to the **Z** axis. Generally, the **W** axis is used with the procedural maps.

Click **Polygon** ▨ on the **Selection** panel and then press **Ctrl+A** to select all polygons. On the **Projection** rollout, click **Box Map** 🎲 and then click again to deactivate.

What just happened?

Here, I have activated the **Polygon** selection mode and then selected all polygons. Then, I have applied box mapping to the selected polygons. Box mapping is best suited for the box shaped objects. When you apply this mapping, 3ds Max maps each polygon to the side of the box gizmo that most closely matches the orientation.

On the **Edit UVs** rollout, click **Open UV Editor** to open the **Edit UVWs** window. Choose **Unfold Mapping** from the **Mapping** menu of the window. The **Unfold Mapping** dialog appears. Click **OK** to accept the default settings and to unfold UVs [see Figure E2].

What just happened?

Here, I have applied the unfold mapping function to the selected polygons. This function removes UV clutter and ensures that polygons do not overlap. This function is available only in the **Polygon** selection mode.

Choose **Pick Texture** from the drop-down located on the top-right corner of the **Edit UVWs** window to open **Material/Map Browser** appears. In the browser, double-click on **Bitmap** from the **Maps | General** rollout. In the **Select Bitmap Image File** dialog, select **cardboard_texture.png** and click **Open**. The **cardboard_texture.png** appears in the **Edit UVWs** window [see Figure E3].

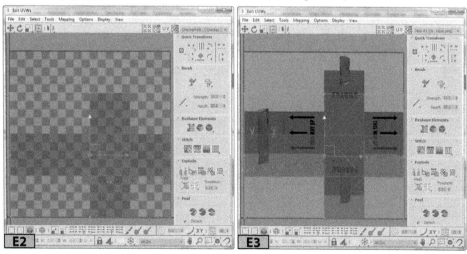

What just happened?

*The **Pick Texture** option allows you to place a map or bitmap in the editor view. You can then use that map or bitmap as a reference for moving UVs.*

Click **Vertex** from the bottom-left corner of the **Edit UVWs** window to activate the **Vertex** selection mode. Notice that all the vertices are selected. If they are not selected, press **Ctrl+A** to select them. Ensure **Move Selected Subobjects** ✛ is active from the **Edit UVWs** window's toolbar and then align all UVs to the background texture [see Figure E4]. Press and hold **Shift** while dragging to constrain the movement.

Now, individually select group of vertices and fine tune the alignment with the background texture [see Figure E5]. You can also select vertices in a viewport. If the UVs are not in a straight line, you can use **Align Horizontally to Pivot** ⁺⁺ and **Align Vertically to Pivot** ⁺⁺ from the **Quick Transform** rollout of the **Edit UVWs** window to straighten the UVs. Close the **Edit UVWs** window.

Press **M** to open **Slate Material Editor**. From the **Material/Map Browser** | **Materials** rollout | **Scanline** rollout, double-click **Standard** to add it to the **Active View** and then assign it to the box in the scene. Rename the material as **boxMat**. Connect **cardboard_texture.png** texture to the **Diffuse** slot of the material. RMB click on **boxMat** node and choose **Show Shaded Material in Viewport** from the menu to display the texture in the viewport.

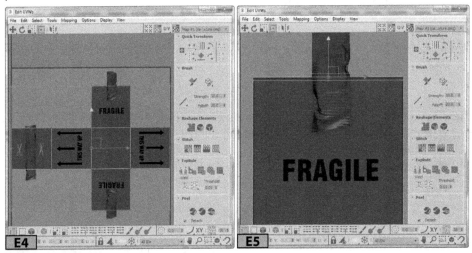

Exercise T7: Texturing a Dice

In this exercise, we will texturing a dice [see Figure E1] using **UV Editor**. In this Exercise we will export the UVs template to the Photoshop and then use Photoshop to create the texture. We will then import the texture back into 3ds Max and will apply it to the dice geometry.

Table ET7 - Texturing a Dice	
Skill level	Intermediate
Time to complete	20 Minutes
Topics in the section	• Getting Ready • Texturing the Dice

Table ET7 - Texturing a Dice	
Project Folder	**unit-mbt**
Final exercise file	**umbt-hoet7-finish.max**

E1

Getting Ready

Reset 3ds Max. Set units to **Generic Units** and then create a box with the **Length, Height**, and **Width** set to **190**.

Texturing the Dice

Ensure the box is selected in a viewport and then go to **Modify** panel. Add the **Unwrap UVW** modifier to the stack. Click **Polygon** ▣ on the **Selection** panel and then press **Ctrl+A** to select all polygons. On the **Projection** rollout, click **Box Map** 📦 and then click again to deactivate.

On the **Edit UVs** rollout, click **Open UV Editor** to open the **Edit UVWs** window. Choose **Unfold Mapping** from the **Mapping** menu of the window. The **Unfold Mapping** dialog appears. Click **OK** to accept the default settings and unfold UVs.

Choose **Render UVW Template** from the **Tools** menu to open the **Render UVs** dialog. Click **Render UV Template** on the dialog. The **Render Map** window appears. Click **Save Image** on the window's toolbar to open the **Save Image** dialog. Type **dice_template** in the **File name** field and choose **PNG Image File** from the **Save as** type drop-down.

Click **Save** to save the template. Click **OK** from the **PNG Configuration** dialog. Now, close all windows and dialogs. Open **dice_template.png** in **Photoshop**. **Layer 0** appears in the **Layers** panel. Create a new layer below **Layer 0** and fill it with **black** [see Figure E2].

Now, using **Photoshop** tools and features create dice texture according to the dice template. I am putting simple numbers to identify the faces of the dice [see Figure E3]. You should go ahead and create a nice looking dice texture for your dice model.

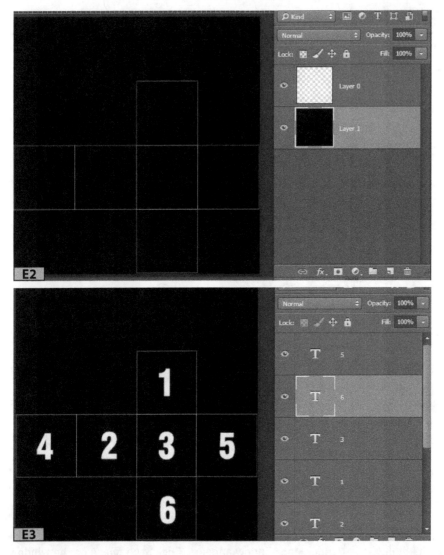

Now, switch off the **black** layer and the **template** layer. Save the **Photoshop** document as **dice_texture.png**.

In 3ds Max, apply a **Standard** material to the box. Set **Diffuse** color to **red**. Connect **dice_texture.png** to the **Diffuse Color** and **Opacity** slots of the material's node, respectively. In the **dice_texture.png** map | **Bitmap Parameters** rollout, turn off the **Premultiplied Alpha** switch. Render the scene.

Appendix A: Quiz Answers

Multiple Choice
1. C, 2. C, 3. A

Fill in the Blanks
1. **Adjustment**, 2. **Masks**, 3. **Difference Clouds**, 4. **High Pass**, 5. **Equalize**, 6. **Levels**

True/False
1. T, 2. T, 3. F

Multiple Choice
1. C, 2. C

Fill in the Blanks
1. **Auto**, 2. **Delete**, 3. **Ctrl+Tab**

True/False
1. F, 2. T, 3. T

Multiple Choice
1. A, 2. D

Fill in the Blanks
1. **SuperSampling**, 2. **Metal**, 3. **Oren-Nayar-Blinn**, 4. **Blend**, 5. **Morpher**, 6. **Multi/Sub-Object**, 7. **Top/Bottom**, 8. **Matte/Shadow**, 9. **Ink 'n Paint**, 10. **UVW Remove**

True/False
1. T, 2. T, 3. F, 4. F, 5. T

Multiple Choice
1. C, 2. C

Fill in the Blanks
1. **ART, Arnold**, 2. 100, 3. **weight**, 4. **IOR**, 5. **Anisotropy**

True/False
1. T, 2. T, 3. F

Unit ML1 - Standard Lights

Multiple Choice
1. D, 2. D

Fill in the Blanks
1. **Shadow Map**, 2. **Ray-traced**, 3. luminance=RO/R, **RO, R, R**, 4. **Show Cone**, 5. **Ray Bias**, 6. **Omni**

True/False
1. F, 2. T, 3. T, 4. T, 5. F, 6. F, 7. T

Unit ML2 - Photometric Lights

Multiple Choice
1. B, 2. D, 3. D

Fill in the Blanks
1. **Look At Controller**, 2. **Exposure**, 3. **HID**

True/False
1. T, 2. T

Unit ML3 - Sunlight and Daylight

Fill in the Blanks
1. **Sunlight**, 2. **System**, 3. **Daylight**, 4. **Sun Positioner**

Index

Symbols

3D Connexion CI2-8

A

Arranging Objects
Arrange command CI2-5
Center command CI2-5
Duplicate command CI2-5

D

Deformer Objects
Bend CM2-29
Bevel CM2-31
Bulge CM2-29
Camera Deformer CM2-30
Collision Deformer CM2-30
Correction CM2-29
Displacer CM2-30
Explosion CM2-29
ExplosionFX CM2-29
FFD CM2-29
Formula CM2-30
Jiggle CM2-29
Melt CM2-29
Mesh Deformer CM2-29
Morph CM2-30
Polygon Reduction CM2-31
Shatter CM2-29
Shear CM2-29
Shrink Wrap CM2-30
Smoothing Deformer CM2-31
Spherify CM2-30
Spline Deformer CM2-30
Spline Rail CM2-30
Spline Wrap CM2-30
Squash and Stretch CM2-29
Surface CM2-30
Taper CM2-29
Twist CM2-29
Wind Deform CM2-31

Wrap CM2-30

G

Generators
Bezier CM1-4
Extrude CM1-4
Lathe CM1-4
Loft CM1-4
Subdivision Surface CM1-4
Sweep CM1-4

I

Important Tools
Annotation Tool CI2-4
Doodle options CI2-7
Guide Tool CI2-1
Lens Distortion tool CI2-6
Lighting Tool CI2-2
Measure & Construction Tool CI2-3
Naming Tool CI2-3
Interface CI1-6
Camera menu [MEV] CI1-9
CINEMA 4D Interface Elements CI1-1
Configure All Viewports CI1-14
Configure Viewport CI1-14
Display menu [MEV] CI1-11
Help CI1-19
  Commander CI1-19
Hidden Menus CI1-20
HUD CI1-15
Menubar CI1-3
Menu in editor view CI1-8
Options menu [MEV] CI1-12
Standard Palette CI1-3
Title Bar CI1-3

M

Managers and Browsers
Attribute Manager CI1-17
Content Browser CI1-18
Coordinate Manager CI1-17
Layer Manager CI1-18
Material Manager CI1-17
Object Manager CI1-15
  Rearranging Objects CI1-16

Structure Manager CI1-18
Take Manager CI1-17
Mesh Menu
Align Normals CM2-18
Array CM2-8
Axis Center CM2-18
Bevel CM2-15
Break Phong Shading CM2-18
Break Segment CM2-21
Bridge CM2-15
Brush CM2-17
Center Object to CM2-19
Center Parent to CM2-19
Center to Parent CM2-19
Chamfer CM2-21
Change Point Order CM2-13
Clone CM2-9
Close Polygon Hole CM2-16
Collapse CM2-9
Connect Objects CM2-8
Connect pobjects+Delete CM2-8
Connect Points/Edges CM2-10
Create Outline CM2-22
Create Point CM2-13
Cross Section CM2-22
Current State to Object CM2-7
Disconnect CM2-9
Dissolve CM2-11
Edge Cut CM2-13
Edge to Spline CM2-12
Equal Tangent Direction CM2-20
Equal Tangent Length CM2-19
Explode Segments CM2-21
Extrude CM2-16
Extrude Inner CM2-16
Hard Interpolation CM2-19
Iron CM2-17
Join Segment CM2-20
Line Cut CM2-14
Line Up CM2-22
Loop/Path Cut CM2-14
Magnet CM2-17
Make Editable CM2-7
Matrix Extrude CM2-16
Melt CM2-10
Mirror CM2-17

Modeling Settings CM2-13
Move Down Sequence CM2-21
Move Up Sequence CM2-21
N-gon Triangulation CM2-18
Normal Move CM2-17
Normal Rotate CM2-17
Normal Scale CM2-17
Optimize CM2-13
Plane Cut CM2-14
Polygon Groups to Objects CM2-8
Polygon Pen CM2-13
Project CM2-23
Remove N-gons CM2-18
Reset Scale CM2-13
Retriangulate N-gons CM2-18
Reverse Normals CM2-18
Reverse Sequence CM2-21
Round CM2-23
Select Broken Phong Edges CM2-18
Set First Point CM2-21
Set Point Value CM2-12
Slide CM2-17
Smooth Shif CM2-16
Soft Interpolation CM2-19
Spin Edge CM2-12
Spline And CM2-24
Spline Intersect CM2-24
Spline Or CM2-24
Spline Subtract CM2-23
Split CM2-9
Stitch and Sew CM2-16
Subdivide CM2-11
Triangulate CM2-11
Unbreak Phong Shading CM2-18
Untriangulate CM2-12
View Center CM2-19
Weight Subdivision Surface CM2-18
Weld CM2-16
Modeling Objects
Array CM2-25
Atom Array CM2-25
Boole CM2-26
Connect CM2-26
Instance CM2-27
Metaball CM2-27
Python Generator CM2-28

Spline Mask CM2-26
Symmetry Object CM2-27
Modes
Center Axis to CM2-19
Edges CM2-2
Points CM2-1
Polygons CM2-2

P

Project Settings CI1-19

R

Render Tools
Edit Render Settings CI1-5
Render to Picture Viewer CI1-5
Render View CI1-5

S

Selection and TransformTools CI1-6
Active Tool CI1-4
Lasso Selection CI1-4
Move Tool CI1-4
Navigation Tools CI1-7
Polygon Selection CI1-4
Rectangle Selection CI1-4
Rotate Tool CI1-4
Scale Tool CI1-4
X-Axis / Heading CI1-4
Y-Axis / Pitch CI1-5
Z-Axis / Bank CI1-5
Selection Tools
Convert Selection CM2-5
Deselect All CM2-3
Fill Selection CM2-3
Grow Selection CM2-4
Hide Selected CM2-4
Hide Unselected CM2-4
Invert CM2-4
Invert Visibility CM2-5
Loop Selection CM2-2
Outline Selection CM2-2
Path Selection CM2-3
Phong Break Selection CM2-3
Ring Selection CM2-2
Select All CM2-3

Select Connected CM2-4
Set Selection CM2-5
Set Vertex Weight CM2-5
Shrink Selection CM2-4
Unhide All CM2-5
Spline Tools
Pen Tool CM1-2
Spline Arch Tool CM1-2
Spline Sketch Tool CM1-1
Spline Smooth Tool CM1-2

V

Virtual Walkthrough
Collision Orbit Tool CI2-8
Virtual Walkthrough Tool CI2-8

W

Workplanes
Align Selection to Workplane tool CI2-5
Align Workplane to Selection tool CI2-5
Align Workplane to X tool CI2-5
Align Workplane to Y tool CI2-5
Align Workplane to Z tool CI2-5
WWW tag CI2-4

This page intentionally left blank

Other Books Published by Rising Polygon

List of Books Published by Rising Polygon

CINEMA 4D Studio

- Beginner's Guide to Create Models With CINEMA 4D R18 Studio
- Shading, Lighting, and Rendering Techniques with CINEMA 4D Studio R18
- Modeling Techniques with CINEMA 4D R17 Studio

3ds Max

- Beginner's Guide to Create Models With 3ds Max 2018
- Modeling Techniques with 3ds Max 2017
- Getting Started with Physical, mental ray, and Autodesk Materials in 3ds Max 2017
- Getting Started with General Materials in 3ds Max 2017
- Texturing Techniques with 3ds Max 2017

3ds Max / CINEMA 4D Combo

- Beginner's Guide to Create Models With 3ds Max 2018 and CINEMA 4D R18 Studio
- Modeling Techniques with 3ds Max 2017 and CINEMA 4D R17 Studio
- Modeling Techniques with 3ds Max 2016 and CINEMA 4D R17 Studio

Free eBooks

- Create Textures and Background Design Patterns with Photoshop
- CG Tutorials Collection

www.ingramcontent.com/pod-product-compliance
Lightning Source LLC
LaVergne TN
LVHW062315060326
832902LV00013B/2236